Journal of South Asian and Middle Eastern Studies

Vol. XL, No. 2
Winter 2017

The *Journal of South Asian and Middle Eastern Studies* is published
by Villanova University, Villanova PA 19085. (610) 519-4791. All
correspondence should be addressed to the Editors: Hafeez.Malik@
villanova.edu or Kail.Ellis@villanova.edu.
Website address: jsames.villanova.edu

The *Journal* is published quarterly, and its annual subscription is $30; U.S.
Institutions: $35; foreign subscription: $40.

Journal of South Asian and Middle Eastern Studies

Vol. XL No. 2   WINTER 2017

Contributions

Articles are invited from all parts of the world. They should be between 2,000 and 6,000 words and in size 12 font, double-spaced, with footnotes and must follow the Chicago Manual of Style. The Journal will be published in English. Articles written in other languages may not be submitted. Submission of an article will be taken to imply that it has not been previously published and is not on offer to any other publisher. Please submit articles via email as an attached Microsoft Word document to hafeez.malik@villanova.edu. Also include a brief three to six line autobiography.

* * *

The major objective of the Journal of South Asian and Middle Eastern Studies is to provide a forum for scholars engaged in study of the modern Islamic and non-Islamic societies in South Asia, the Middle East, and North Africa. It hopes to create a dialogue among specialists and leaders in public affairs in a wide range of areas and disciplines. The physical sciences, the biological sciences, the social sciences, business administration, public administration and the arts and humanities will be included. Special issues might concentrate on such topics as regional cooperation, religious and intellectual developments, public works, engineering advances, and the impact of transnational cooperation on national communities.

The Journal welcomes contributions, not only from scholars, but also from leaders in public affairs. Editorial policy avoids commitment to any political viewpoint or ideology, but invites discussion of these issues in the modern context on the understanding that all responsibility for opinions expressed, and accuracy of facts, rests exclusively with the author and not with the Journal or its Editor or the Editorial Board.

Articles appearing in this Journal are abstracted and indexed in HISTORICAL ABSTRACTS and AMERICA: HISTORY AND LIFE.

EDITORIAL FOREWORD

Symbols are powerful political tools often used to claim rights, mobilize groups, and legitimize various actions. We understand our political world and shape our decisions in large part by assigning meanings to objects, and persons. All over the world, including the Middle East, political messages are communicated through slogans, banners, festivals, statues, gestures, and ritual acts. In the day to day political processes, the symbolic power of signs is converted into political power. In contrast to its increasing role in various decision making processes, however, political symbolism in the Middle East continues to receive inadequate scholarly attention. This special issue of Political Symbolism in the Middle East examines the symbolic aspects of politics in the Middle East, both historically and in contemporary discourse.

The first article focus on "Constructing a High-Society Mosque: The Controversy and Significance of the Şakirin Mosque in Istanbul, Turkey" Yücel Demirer discusses the unique construction process of the Şakirin Mosque in Istanbul, Turkey and the controversies associated with its construction. Looking beyond form and function, which are known as the principal characteristics of architectural design, this paper intends to analyze the representation of contemporary religious standpoints in Turkey through the Şakirin Mosque's design and construction process. Closely reviewing the architectural characteristics of this "high society mosque" and discussing the interior designer's extensive exercise of freedom in her choice of forms and motifs, he elaborates the ways in which the design negotiates issues of national and religious identity and the major controversies that influence religious discourses in Turkey.

Focusing on the use of colors, in seven short stories written by Libyan writer and political activist Azza Al-Maghour during the uprising and immediately after the war, Safa Elnaili's article "Fighting Oppression with Colors in Libyan Short Story Post the Arab Spring: A Stylistics Analysis of Azza Al-Maghour`s Short Stories" explores the development of language style in showcasing socio-political resistance in the Arab Spring. The analysis suggests the use of the same colors in literary works as a resistance to the regime and displays Libyan authors` styles to fight censorship, political oppression, and social injustice in their literary works.

Javier Gil Guerrero's article "A Stage for the Revolution: Muharram and the Paradigm of Karbala in the context of Khomeini's Struggle with the Shah" moves us to Iran and the appropriation of tradition in contemporary politics. Based upon the significant religious ceremonies of Iran, he analyzes Khomeini's interpretation of the martyrdom of Imam Hussein and his use of

1

the mourning of Muharram in his confrontation with the Pahlavis. Guerrero argues that by framing Hussein's story within a revolutionary framework of a fight against tyranny and oppression, Khomeini altered the significance of important rituals in Shia Islam like Tazieh to advance an activist interpretation of Islam.

Referring to the discourse of modernity/backwardness, in an attempt to categorize modern Persian novels for their functional motifs, in his article titled "The Role of the Discourse of Modernity/Backwardness in Motifs of Modern Persian Fictions" Saeed Honarmand examines these texts in relation to the political and cultural solutions that have been offered by political activists. He argues that although "revealing ignorance" the motif that most Persian fiction has been constructed around still exist, some writers are seeking other possibilities in new discourses, such as in new definitions of law and women's rights.

In "Sa'adallah Wannus's Munamnamaat Tarikhiyah (Historical Miniatures): The Question of History and Role of the Intellectual," Nezar Andary studies how Sa'adallah Wannus reexamines well known historical event and symbol of Ibn Khaldun to define the role of intellectual in society. He highlights that while Wannus' play becomes a foundational text for intellectuals of the postcolonial world that advocates a new vision of national identity and the revaluation of the position of the intellectual provokes a cultural intervention that imagines a new way of confronting history and historiography itself.

The final article focus on Arab and Jewish editorial cartoons in the first half of the twentieth century. Jeff Barnes' article, "Another Sharp Weapon: Gender and Revolt in Arab and Jewish Editorial Cartoons, 1936-39" looks at the significant role of the cartoons in producing public opinion in the perennial emerging conflict in Palestine from the gender perspective. While exploring how these cartoons demonstrate the degree to which nationalist discourse was gendered during the Palestinian revolt and reveal the utility of the editorial cartoon for understanding this period, Barnes suggests that the cartoons provided an important medium through which emerging notions of Palestinian and Jewish identity could be negotiated during the transformative events of 1936-39.

Yücel Demirer (visiting editor)

Constructing a High-Society Mosque: The Controversy and Significance of the Sakirin Mosque in Istanbul, Turkey

Yücel Demirer*

This article addresses the unique construction process of the Şakirin Mosque, located near Karacaahmet Cemetery in the Anatolian section of Istanbul, Turkey, and the controversies associated with its construction. Looking beyond form and function, which are known as the principal characteristics of architectural design, this article analyzes the representation of contemporary religious standpoints in Turkey through the Şakirin Mosque's design and construction process. The mosque was funded by the children of a prominent philanthropist couple and designed by the team of a prominent mosque architects and a female interior designer who has won awards for her work including bars and restaurants. This striking and spacious structure has sparked controversy in Turkey and became known to journalists as "the high society mosque." Closely reviewing the architectural characteristics of the mosque and discussing the interior designer's extensive exercise of freedom in her choice of forms and motifs, this essay intends to elaborate the ways in which the design negotiates issues of national and religious identity. In the process of this analysis, the major controversies that influence religious discourses in Turkey come to light.

* Yücel Demirer received his Ph.D. from Ohio State University and is a member of Kocaeli Academy for Solidarity in Turkey. His research centers on the intersection of culture and politics. He has published articles and books on political culture, symbolic politics and political aspects of religion.

An earlier version of this paper was presented in the Annual Meeting of the American Academy of Religion, San Francisco, CA, on November 19th 2011. The author would like to thank Nicole Wilkinson Duran for her helpful and constructive comments that significantly contributed to improving final version of the paper. Email: yuceldemirer@gmail.com

. . .

Lindsay Jones, prominent architectural historian of worship places, reminds us that a building's meaning can be categorized as "situational, provisional and non-definitive," and that, like other artistic works, buildings convey a plurality of meanings.[1] However, Jones also assures us that "[a]rchitecture is definitely the most visible and arguably the most powerful means both for expressing and for stimulating religious sensibilities."[2] The varieties of architecture and decoration in places of worship and the side-by-side analysis of objects and styles has occupied a significant position in scholarly research. Scholars interested in the interplay between religion and social change have examined the material and cultural aspect of worship places for a long time. In keeping with this research, the present essay focuses on the case of the Şakirin Mosque from the perspective of material culture and architecture. The mosque forms a noteworthy site for this kind of study for two reasons. First, we will see that the mosque's design functions to display the social transformation and negotiation between the main social and political divisions in Turkey. Second, by bringing artists, architects, and various other practitioners together, the Şakirin project has functioned as a material bridge in a highly divided context. The Şakirin Mosque symbolizes the negotiations between religious traditions and the laicist sphere in a highly compartmentalized social setting. It further serves as a venue for the invention of a new tradition that would combine conflicting stances together. While bridging different lifestyles throughout the construction process, this project represents tolerance and mutual understanding. The theme of bridging and negotiation is the focal point of analysis. Manifold interactions among various bitterly divided actors and social groups occur within Şakirin's architecture and decoration. In contrast to some divisive mosque projects in Turkey,[3] Şakirin will be discussed as a harmonizing project that may stand as an answer to the growing controversy over mosques in Turkey and as a pragmatic solution in negotiations among opposing social positions.

With its religious, aesthetic, and historic importance, this project also paved the way for the purpose-built mosques which correlate the issue of meaning at the personal level. While this study is very much interested in the display of multi-layered meanings of Şakirin for different parties, informal

---

[1] Lindsay Jones, *The Hermeneutics of Sacred Architecture*, Vol. 1, (Cambridge, Massachusetts: Harvard University Press, 2000), 34.

[2] Lindsay Jones, "Eventfulness of Architecture: Teaching about Sacred Architecture is Teaching about Ritual," in *Teaching Ritual*, ed. Catherine Bell, (New York: Oxford University Press, 2007), 251.

[3] See. Sefa Şimşek, Zerrin Polvan and Tayfun Yeşilyurt, "The Mosque as a Divisive Symbol in the Turkish Political Landscape," *Turkish Studies*, Vol. 7, No. 3, (2006): 489–508.

everyday practices attached to the mosque and common to all will also be examined. This article also addresses the question of how Şakirin embodies and reflects particular and somewhat new religious ideals and beliefs. Based on interviews and onsite observations, I evaluate the discourses produced through the material elements and the relation between personal experience and institutional tendencies.

Historical Background

After a four-year construction period, the so called "most modern mosque" in Turkey, Şakirin, was opened in Istanbul in 2009. The word "Şakirin" refers to the name of the family which supported the construction of the mosque. At the same time the family name is derived from the Arabic word, "şakir," meaning "thankful." Ms. Emine Erdoğan, wife of then prime minister and current president, participated in the opening ceremony for the mosque, addressing the audience and thanking those who were instrumental in the progress of the project. Other significant figures from the religious scene and the central and local governments, such as then the Director of Religious Affairs, Dr. Ali Bardakoğlu and the mayor of Istanbul, Dr. Kadir Topbaş were also present.[4]

Şakirin Mosque was designed by Hüsrev Tayla, a well known mosque architect and architectural conservationist, and built on the site provided by the Istanbul Metropolitan Municipality. The interior designer of the project was Zeynep Fadıllıoğlu, widely known for her award-winning interior designs of extravagant bars and restaurants. Fadıllıoğlu is known as the first female interior designer of a mosque.[5] Despite its relatively small size, the mosque caught public attention.. With its boldly spacious women's section, an artistic fountain in the courtyard, sizeable windows, acrylic *minbar*, a large chandelier, and decorative motifs of Seljuk art, the Şakirin Mosque has generated a great deal of interest.

Noted among the numerous newspaper, magazine, and professional magazine articles written about Şakirin, the mosque even made the March 2011 issue of Forbes Life Magazine with a lavishly illustrated article in which the Şakirin Mosque is described as a "high society" mosque.[6] Seeing a contemporary mosque featured in such a high end and western secular consumer publication is something quite striking.

Aside from the artistic aspects, the "worldly" dimensions of the project were also unique. For instance, the mosque has an exhibition area where artistic

---

[4] http://www.ibb.gov.tr/en-US/Haberler/Pages/Haber.aspx?NewsID=116 (Accessed 1 August 2016).

[5] Designboom. 3 December 2014. http://www.designboom.com/architecture/interview-zeynep-fadillioglu-female-architect-turkey-mosque-12-03-2014/ (Accessed 1 August 2016).

[6] Forbes coverage was kindly brought to my attention by Professor David Simonowitz after my presentation of the first version of this paper in San Francisco.

exhibitions are organized--an unusual feature in a Turkish mosque. Although the popular naming of the mosque as "high-society mosque," or "the most modern mosque" made it of interest to this research, the pop culture feel of its coverage in news, the accompanying uproar, and the attendance of such high level guests at the opening ceremony might have guaranteed that the mosque would be ignored by serious scholars. (However, for my own research, it was impossible not to pay attention to the life stories of Semiha and İbrahim Şakir, in whose memory the mosque was erected.)

When Semiha Şakir passed away at the age of 93 on September 10, 1998 she had already supported a number of major projects, including health clinics, schools, and homes for the elderly.[7] After losing her father in Dardanelles Campaign – Çanakkale Wars, she spent the early years of her life in the upscale housing complex, "Tayyare Apartmanı" in what was an upper class neighborhood of Laleli, in İstanbul. When Istanbul-based relatives of the Saudi bachelor businessman İbrahim Şakir let him know about this beautiful young woman, he came to İstanbul to see her. After a two-year engagement period, they married and settled in Beirut when she was 20. While living with her husband and three children in a palace that once made the cover of Life Magazine, or in a mansion on the banks of the Nile, or in a palace in Mecca, or in a big house in London, she never forgot her native Turkey. She began to make systematic donations to support the constructions of mosques, hospitals, and day-care centers in Turkey as early as the late 1930s.[8]

Throughout these years, she became known as "mother" in Turkey. She also had a reputation as a religious woman with a great respect for Mustafa Kemal Atatürk, the founder and the first president of the Turkish Republic, and for his secular reforms. She was then a true Muslim female philanthropist, native of Turkey, wife of a Saudi businessman, supporter of the modern regime, spending her whole life in the Middle East. In a country where the definition of "modern" has been left to the secular elite, outside of the religious realm for a long time, this couple's life story and the construction of a "modern mosque" to honor their endeavor stands as a perfect venue for negotiation between the religious and the secular point of views in contemporary Turkey.

This claim might easily be considered overreaching. However, as learned from Lily Kong's argument,[9] religion cannot be fully problematized without paying

---

[7] İlnur Çevik considers her as the Turkish version of Mother Teresa. See. http://www.hurriyetdailynews.com/commentaries.aspx?pageID=438&n=commentaries-1998-09-12 Hürriyet Daily News. 12 September 1998. (Accessed 13 July 2016).

[8] For the list of her services and her life story see http://www.hurriyet.com.tr/gozlerini-mutlu-kapadi-39037679 Hürriyet "11 September 1998. (Accessed 13 July 2016).

[9] Lily Kong, "Mapping 'New' Geographies of Religion: Politics and Poetics in Modernity," *Progress in Human Geography*, Vol. 25, No. 2, (2001): 211–233.

attention to the associated cultural geography. It should be remembered that the modern Turkish state building process and the culture attached to it was in part a comprehensive response to the challenges of socio-economic change and modernity beginning from the 19th century. It took the form of a radical, state-engineered cultural revolution, especially in the 1920s. Advancements of that era were felt as part of a conflict between the traditional and the modern, the local and the international, The East and the West, the religious and the secular. Within that historical context, people had a feeling of delay, of having been left behind by the West. The religion of Islam and the religious culture were considered a main source of backwardness. In this first era of Turkey's modern existence, to be modern and educated was to be secular and westernized; from the alphabet to the calendar to clothing, traditional culture that had gone hand in hand with Muslim practice was replaced with secular culture, shaped in large part by the culture of Europe. All forms of being modern were structured outside of the religious realm and any reference to traditional culture and historical Islamic continuity were disparaged.

In the first decade of the republican period, religious dynamics were limited to the private sphere, especially within households. From the 1950s on, however, religion gained some visibility in public life, as well as in the political sphere. Since the military coup of 1980, when the nationalist version of Islam was supported against the "communist threat," there has been a significant increase in Islamic discourse. The privatization campaigns of the 1980s provided a convenient social platform for Islamists, followed by the 2002 political victory of the Justice and Development Party, the ruling party in Turkey today. In the early 2000s a new version of modern life emerged. Traditional ways of being Muslim have been radically modified. Educated and cultured aspects of Muslim identity were consciously highlighted. A segment of the population who are relatively affluent, urban, and well-educated have embraced Islam as part of their social identity. In contrast to the past, where the most vital aspects of being religious were kept in the household, Islamic identities began to be widely and rather proudly expressed in the public domain. The rise of religious conservatism overlapped with a gradual increase in the dominance of Islamic identities in the public sphere.

Although these developments were perceived as a threat to republican ideals and considered by the secular elite the first steps to the creation of an Islamic state, during this time, Islamists in Turkey preferred to occupy a somewhat unexpected position. First, referring to the principles of free speech and democracy, they claimed an equal position in social and political life. Second, instead of challenging the whole modernist and Western way of defining civilization, Islamists redefined these principles, including secularism, according to their beliefs. As part of an effort to gain the consent of secular sectors of Turkey, as well as of the Western world, a symbolic politics was employed. "By resurfacing and inscribing local, traditional, and Islamic symbols (of both past and present) in the most central and favorite urban places," notes a significant analysis, "they demand recognition and legitimacy for their identity."[10]

The case presented in this article can be considered part of this effort for recognition and legitimacy as well as in keeping with the non-stop competition for the possession of modernist ideals by religious conservatives in Turkey. Therefore, when the children of a Saudi businessman - a bold representation of the East and of the Muslim world- and a secular minded Turkish woman – the gender façade of modern Turkey - supported the construction of a "modern mosque," it became a suitable negotiation site for the social and political needs of the 21st century Turkey, in which religion has always been and remains a conflicted issue.

What is observed in this project is the systematic re-claiming of modern elite status by Islamists—a status that the secular republican elite has monopolized since the foundation of the Turkish Republic. The "mute text" of the mosque not only challenges the domination of the written text, but also expands the understanding of the conflict-laden religious setting, by providing an alternative vehicle of knowledge.

The Şakirin Mosque was not the first controversial mosque project to take place in Istanbul. In 2005, for instance, two controversial mosque projects for Göztepe Park and Taksim Square created major controversy, being seen as an Islamist attempt to subjugate the political arena. However, there are many reasons to consider the case of Şakirin as the start of a new sort of dialogue. This time the discourse that re-claims the modernist position has been more eloquent and indirect. The subtlety of Şakirin's symbolism reminds us of Gadamer's definition of the "symbolic," based upon Heidegger's "pandemic interwovenness of disclosure and hiddenness," a kind of symbolism which is half-revealed and half-concealed.[11]

Artistic Style and the Difference

The uniqueness of the project and its capacity for indirect ways of telling starts with the beauty and impressiveness of the building. Whether one is religious or not, educated or uneducated, male or female, young or old, there is something magnetic in this effort that attracts attention. Next to the historical Karacaahmet Cemetery, the charming Şakirin Mosque gives one an idea of difference at the outset, reminding us of "architecture as both set and player in

---

[10] Şimşek et al., (2006): 504.
[11] cited in Jones, (2000): 22-23.

8

the ongoing theatre of social life."[12]

The fountain located in the courtyard, on the way to the inside of the building, is not the traditional kind that can be seen in the majority of the mosques in Turkey. Rather, this is a very modern looking fountain, designed by the British artist William Pye, located in the centre of the courtyard. The fountain's surface acts as a mirror, reflecting the image of the mosque entrance. After this surprising entrance, the main elements of the mosque design welcome the visitor with additional revelations.

The outer walls are a combination of glass and iron pattern, providing openness and clarity. Gilded inscriptions from the Quran are located on the surrounding glass walls. The use of glass is not a common practice in the mosques in Turkey.

[12] Gray Read, "Introduction: The Play's the Thing," in *Architecture as a Performing Art*, ed. Marcia Feuerstein and Gray Read, (Burlington, VT: Ashgate, 2016): 1.

In particular, the eloquent use of glass in three sides of this building is one of its most significant aspects. In our interview, the transparency of the building was the very first point that was highlighted by the imam of Şakirin, Nurullah Çelebi.[13] Eager to put the Şakirin mosque into a historical context, Imam Çelebi positions it within the third phase of mosque architecture, consisting of contemporary work that advances the tradition in modern forms. According to Çelebi, the first phase is the "good old days" marked by the Ottoman ancestors. This phase was followed by the second period in which the good past had been poorly imitated. In this sense, the Şakirin mosque seems to be a revival of the revered past, in a form compatible with the modern world. He explained the preference for this transparency from the walls to the cabinets, where the copies of the Quran and prayer beads are kept, as a reflection of the transparency of the soul: "Just like human beings, the buildings need to be transparent. Our belief is free of hypocrisy and this is a way to convey this belief."

Fadıllıoğlu's unique design shows forth in her interpretation of particular, traditional elements of the mosque. The mihrab, for example, is the semicircular niche that points toward the direction of Mecca and is considered the central

point in the house of worship. In the Şakirin mosque, the mihrab consists of a golden center surrounded by a turquoise arch and constitutes one of the most artistic elements of the structure. Another of the most eloquent aspects of the interior design is the minbar, a pulpit in the mosque where the *imam* stands while delivering sermons. Made out of acrylic with delicate leaf patterns suggestive of calligraphy, the ivory colored minbar sweeps in a dramatic upward curve, the exquisite conception and fine implementation of a deep religious tradition that forms a magnetic focal point for worshippers.

Suspended above the praying area is an expansive chandelier composed of intersecting circles of light. While making newcomers look up in the building and creating a second focal point in the room, it also provides a sophisticated look. At the personal level, despite its size and brilliance, the lighting's effect is one of tranquility. These aspects of Şakirin on the one hand mark a modern awakening of the mosque architecture that may be said to have suffered and collapsed in Turkey previously. These artistic

---

[13] This interview with imam Nurullah Çelebi was conducted in October 2011 after several visits to the mosque.

10

innovations mean a fresh start after decades of second class copies of Ottoman architecture. The team of artists is collectively changing the scene by putting contemporary touches on the structure. However, besides these artistic aspects, there are some worldly and non-artistic issues that need to be addressed here.

In her 2003 study on the 19th century Connecticut Western Reserve, titled "Moral Geography: Maps, Missionaries, and the American Frontier," Amy DeRogatis argues that the missionaries work "was not simply (or often) to convert souls, but to define religious identity by articulating the relationship between spatial and moral values on the frontier."[14] Keeping DeRogatis point in mind, in the following section, I will present and discuss Şakirin's additional function for the re-definition and articulation of contemporary Muslim identity in the socially divided context of Turkey.

First of all, we need to consider the women's section of the Şakirin Mosque. Although there is no written rule available, the Muslim worshippers are supposed to pray in different locations according to gender differences. Traditionally women have practiced their belief in a special section of the mosques, generally located in the back rows, behind the men. In a significant number of cases women pray in secondary rooms, sometimes in small dark places in front of the shelves where shoes are kept, away from the main halls. Indeed, in some cases women are not allowed in the mosque at all, due to the lack of divided space. Considering this tendency and the given background, the Şakirin's women's

---

[14] Amy DeRogatis, *Moral Geography: Maps, Missionaries, and the American Frontier*, (New York: Columbia University Press, 2003).

section requires special attention.

In Şakirin, the women's section is located in a big balcony which is located on an entresol or mezzanine. The upper position of the section does not only provide a clear and unobstructed view of the hall, it also provides the women's congregation with a somewhat predominant position in the hall. By paying more attention to this habitually neglected section, Fadıllıoğlu and her team are voicing one of the most significant messages to the religious old guard as well as the secular part of the Turkish population about gender equality. This fresh and strong message definitely challenges the traditional way of thinking and highlights the need for a more equal position for the women.

As discussed throughout this paper, numerous international artists as well as artists from Turkey who have never worked in similar projects were employed for the Şakirin mosque. In this religiously divided society, the design team consisted of people from different lifestyles and spheres of the society. When the artists were interviewed by the national and international media representatives, some controversial points of views were made public. For instance, Fadıllıoğlu stated that she "cares more of the aesthetic side" of her work. Similarly, Nahide Büyükkaymakçı's, the designer of the chandelier, told reporters that she was "not really a practicing Muslim."[15]

These and other issues were brought to a conversation with Nurullah Çelebi, the imam of Şakirin, who responded in a thoughtful and thought-provoking manner. Çelebi is a man of small stature with sharp looking eyes. A soft spoken,

---

[15] Hürriyet Daily, 23 May 2009 http://www.hurriyet.com.tr/unlikely-mosque-designer-wows-with-reverent-stunner-11707701 (Accessed 2 July 2016).

well-mannered, and educated man, he is the second imam of the mosque. Since he has lived in Üsküdar from the age of 12, he is familiar with the history of Şakirin. When I first entered his office in the courtyard of Şakirin, I was puzzled as to whether I needed to take off my shoes, which is required in the praying hall. He noticed my hesitation and told me that I need not. In this very Western office, instead of sitting in his chair behind his desk, he preferred to sit directly across from me. In a modest tone, he informed me about his religious education and the previous posts that he had occupied. He was comfortable while responding to my, sometimes sensitive, questions. He highlighted the importance of Şakirin as one of the two neighborhood mosques where women can conduct Eid Prayer. He expressed as well his sense that Şakirin Mosque is a middle ground between nearby Zeynep Kamil Women's and Children's Hospital and Karacaahmet Cemetery: "We enter the world through Zeynep Kamil Hospital and leave it from Karacaahmet and in the middle here is Şakirin."

When I asked about the inclusion of secular artists such as Büyükkaymakçı and Fadıllıoğlu in the construction and design of the mosque, Çelebi responded to my questions eloquently. In addition to making some positive comments about the talent of women for the artistic arena, the imam described his own sense of the connection between the artist and the sacred:

> Every human being intends to leave an impact behind her/him to seek Allah's consent. This might be a book, an artistic work as in the case of examples that you mentioned. First we need to consider this human need. Second, Allah is beautiful and loves and deserves beauty. When the decision needed to be made for the various artistic tasks, the best of their expertise was needed. Nobody was interested in how Muslim they were or how they lived. There is an *ayah* (chapter) in the Quran, Surat An-Nisa reads 'Indeed, Allah commands you to render trust to whom it is due and when you judge between people to judge with justice. Excellent is that which Allah instructs you. Indeed, Allah is ever Hearing and Seeing.' Therefore, the Şakirin family was just interested in finding the best, and that was all. Moreover, the designers consulted theologians on a regular basis. I would also like to tell you something that your question reminded me of. While a French TV channel was interviewing me and Fadıllıoğlu together, I brought up an historical account on Umm Umarah's defense of the Prophet Muhammad in the Battle of Uhud and her skill with the sword in the battle of this Muslim woman from the famous Banu Najjar tribe. This story made Fadıllıoğlu cry. I believe there is something inside these artists for Allah.

Finally, I must say something about an area that I did not expect would be relevant. When in the field, I try not to be an armchair researcher. Consistent with this preference, I wanted to see the restroom facilities of the Şakirin Mosque, as well as the place for ablutions. When I entered the restroom, near the ablution fountain, my main interest was to see a modern version of the facilities for the given purpose. However, when I saw the urinals in this section I was surprised. Considering the classification of human waste as impure, there are certain rules by which Muslims may relieve themselves properly. For many Muslims relieving oneself while standing is considered a sin. Although there are many restroom facilities with urinals in Turkey, a significant number of mosques purposely function with no urinals. When I asked Imam Çelebi's take on this, first he explained the reasoning of the limitations on this human need-- the loss of personal modesty and the increase in impurity. However, he continued by saying that; "worshippers are not the only ones who come to Şakirin. They need to be free to relieve themselves in the way they prefer. Also there is no room for any kind of coercion in our religion."

In keeping with this preference against coercion, I noticed a similar example from the women's section. As you see in the figure there is a small closet with women clothing in it. This very well organized and well-maintained closet is full of head scarves and skirts, to be used by the visitors. I need to clarify that in some older mosques, this type of apparel is kept for the tourists as well as for those female visitors who are not prepared. However, in most mosques these items gather dust and wrinkles to become fairly unappealing; quite the contrary was the case in Şakirin. The contrast suggests that a strong effort has been made to accommodate the comfort as well as the decorum of a variety of female visitors.

The comparison with the urinals here is interesting. In the men's restrooms, men who choose not to follow the religious tradition of sitting while relieving themselves are allowed to stand. Provision is made for these men—non-Muslims or Muslims who are not strict on this particular instruction--to effectively transgress the preferred tradition. In the case of the women, however, a provision is made for women who arrive unprepared to keep the tradition of modesty nonetheless--by covering their heads with the scarves provided and their legs with the generous skirts provided. These women might be non-Muslims, non-practicing Muslims, or perhaps less traditional Muslim women who arrive unprepared for the visit. The thoughtful, generous accommodation for them is striking. In other mosques, the dusty, untended scarves and skirts give visiting women the impression that beggars cannot be choosers—women who come unprepared must take what they can get. To tend to the needs of visiting women as is done in the Sakirin Mosque implies that the unprepared or not-fully-acculturated are welcomed and expected. On the other hand, the provision of clean and nicely cared for garments indicates that the traditional expectation of modesty still stands, and applies to first-time visitors as well as regulars.

In Lieu of Conclusion

Why does the design of a mosque matter? How do we analyze the relationship between religious culture and materiality? What do we make of the observations recorded here? Architecture has often emerged from and expressed religious commitment, but at the very same time religious architecture has the capacity to shape meaning, culture, and religious practice as well as belief. As part of a response to the secular modernist discourse, the Şakirin Mosque attains an alternative modern position for both the religious and the non-religious parts of society. Henri Lefebvre reminds us to be alert to shifting meanings of the text: ". . . a monumental work [of architecture], like a musical one, does not have a 'signified' (or 'signifieds'); rather, it has a horizon of meaning: a specific or indefinite multiplicity of meanings, a shifting hierarchy in which now one, now another meaning comes momentarily to the fore, by means of – and for the sake of – a particular action."[16]

What I have suggested here is that different components of the Turkish society have interacted and move toward a new tone for the future of society through the construction process of this mosque. Considering public space as a territory contested between the secular and the religious segments of society, we have looked at some ways in which these negotiations are realized. However, neither the secular nor the religious position can be understood without reference to the process of Turkish nation building and the "thick description" beneath it.[17]

The Şakirin Mosque project fulfilled three related but somewhat different functions. Şakirin, first, acts as a concrete representation of the modern Islamic

---

[16] cited in Jones, (2000): 22-23.
[17] Clifford Geertz, "Thick Description: Toward an Interpretive Theory of Culture," in *The Interpretation of Cultures: Selected Essays*, (New York: Basic Books, 1973): 3-30.

view. While expressing the values from the past, by combining unconventional artistic sources, it also looks to the future. Şakirin picks up on motifs from the history of mosque architecture, such as the use of calligraphy and light within the design, and adheres to elements required by the tradition—the minbar, the domed ceiling, the women's section. These aspects of the tradition lead the worshipper forward into the future indicated by the new materials, new aspects of design, and a reclaimed and renewed aesthetic that resounds more boldly in the contemporary world. Thus to be in the mosque is to be in touch with both an ancient tradition and an intellectual and aesthetic cutting edge movement. Using contemporary design and materials, the structure creates within it a contemporary, sleek, urban, and educated Islam. The mosques of previous decades in Turkey copied Ottoman traditions, with lesser materials and a reduced emphasis on aesthetics. These structures were meant to invoke religious tradition, not to carve out a new social place for religion. Şakirin, on the other hand, seems designed to proclaim that Islam is not only alive in its Turkish setting, but that it can stand once again as a leader of the culture as a whole.

Secondly, responding to the ideal of gender equality inherent in modern western thinking, the mosque provides a more equal position to women. Without changing old customs, it seems to accommodate women coming from the secular world and to imply that women are valued within contemporary Islam. The prominent place of the women's section in the mosque seems designed to argue that women within Islam may be set apart from men, but are not thus devalued. Given that traditional modesty for women has become (within Turkey and elsewhere) the most visible difference between gender roles within and outside of Islam, the care given to provision of modest garments in Şakirin is significant. A selection of clean, appealing and even fashionable garments with which visiting women can cover themselves makes an eloquent statement about the desirability of Muslim modesty (and of Islam generally) and the ease of transition to it from secular forms of dress. Since secular objections to Muslim tradition often focus on gender issues, this softening of gender roles and attention to women has the effect of answering an unspoken, secular objection.

Third, besides its various functions in worship, Şakirin also stand as a repositories of symbolic meaning for modern ideas. In other words, it stands as a response to the question of "in what architectural and stylistic idiom can a mosque be created in modern Turkey?" Turkey's cultural geography is full of historical and contemporary data to support a determination in this nature and thus require close readings of mosque production processes. In his excellent book *Theology in Stone: Church Architecture from Byzantium to Berkeley*, Richard Kieckhefer uses the structures of the churches and the objects used in them to understand the changes in thinking and prioritizations in religious traditions.[18] Through the spatial configurations and the use of sacred objects and other forms of religious representation in the carefully chosen case studies, he successfully demonstrates the main theological emphases and shifts. Although there is no theological shift in the case of Şakirin, the visual evidence of various aspects suggests new meanings within this sacred place. The unique aspect of the Şakirin project is that in many ways the details of this construction process reminds us of mosques in the Western world, designed for co-existence with people of other faiths. Like these western mosques and unlike more conventional mosques in Turkey, Şakirin seems eager to converse with outsiders, Muslim and otherwise. Rather than claiming a space isolated from contemporary civic concerns, the Şakirin mosque negotiates those concerns and defines the conversation its own way.

---

[18] Richard Kieckhefer, *Theology in Stone: Church Architecture from Byzantium to Berkeley,* (New York: Oxford University Press, 2004).

Fighting Oppression with Colors in Libyan Short Story Post The Arab Spring: A Stylistics Analysis of Azza Al-Maghour`s Short Stories

Safa Elnaili*

Introduction

Libya's four decades of dictatorship and oppression put Libyan writers and authors under censorship for many years. They struggled with Qaddafi's regime and were constantly punished for expressing their opinions regarding the dogmatic rule and the poor economic conditions of the oil country. According to Fagih,[1] the leading character in Libyan short stories is mostly a simple man struggling daily to survive hardship and oppression, or a helpless woman suffering social inequality according to Alhaddad.[2]

Nevertheless, many of these writers and fiction authors adopted certain language and literary styles in order to channel their thoughts to their readers. Implicit writing and cultural metaphors were among their main literary styles. A study by Elnaili[3] analyzed several Libyan short stories published during Qaddafi's rule of Libya; the study revealed that Libyan authors relied heavily

---

[1]*Safa Elnaili is an Assistant Professor in Arabic Language and Literature at the Modern She taught Intermediate Arabic in the Foreign Languages Department and an Arabian Nights Seminar in The International Studies Department at Louisiana State University. Her Research interests are: Libyan Literature, Modern Arabic Literature, Translation Theory & Practice, Critical Discourse Analysis, The Arabian Nights, and SLA.

[2] Ahmed Fagih, *The Libyan Short Story: A Research and Anthology* (United States: Xlibiris Corporation, 2008).

[2] Fawzi Alhaddad, *Critical Studies in Libyan Narrative* (Benghazi: Dar Alkutub Alwataniya, 2010).

[3] Safa Elnaili, "Adjectives of Colour in Libyan Short Stories: A Stylistic Analysis." in *Language, Literature and Style in Africa*, ed. Arua E. Arua, Taiwo Abioye, & Kehinde A. Ayoola, 131-141 (Cambridge Scholars Publishing, 2014).

on the use of colors and their connotative cultural meanings to represent and discuss certain socio-political issues in the Libyan society. Most of these stories paint the layman as powerless and helpless in the face of the regime's iron fist. However, with the 2011 uprising and the political change that swept the Arab region, writers gained more freedom of criticism and more space for expression.

This article discusses the negative effect of the oppressive history in Libya on its literature, the radical change of the Arab Spring on Libyan creative writing during the revolution, the cultural meanings of colors and how their connotations contribute as a language/ literary style in Libyan short story, Libyan writer Azza Al-Maghour and seven selected stories, an analysis of the effect of use of colors in showing resistance to dictatorship, and finally a conclusion of the study's findings.

Libyan Literature before the Arab Spring

Libya's strategic location as a gate between North Africa and South Europe caused the state to undergo centuries of colonization and wars. Starting from the Ottoman Empire (1551-1911), following it the cruel Italian invasion (1911-1943), and the dictatorship of Qaddafi (1969-2011), all these many years of foreign and domestic oppression kept locals in constant fight with the suppressor to gain freedom and stability. This unsettledness prevented Libyan citizens from developing their society socially and economically and keep pace with the world.

The political unrest, as a result, affected the growth of modern Libyan literature. After Libya declared independence in 1951[4] a number of magazines and newspapers featured some literary works by a few Libyan writers like Wahbi Al- Bouri, other literary works were published abroad, mostly, in Egypt. After independence, the state experienced a major socio-political reform after many years of war and poverty; Literary works reached a high peak of production and this era was considered the Golden Age of Libyan literary works and journalism.[5] Libyan writers were mostly addressing nationalism and the society's social issues like social inequality.

With the overthrown of the Monarchy in 1969 by Qaddafi, Libyan writers clashed with the regime and suffered extreme dominance over free expression especially during the 1980's. Creativity in literary works took a different curve and lowered its tone. Several writers were imprisoned and others were even killed. The style of writing changed; there were no longer daring and challenging characters, Libyan writers used implicit writing styles and indirect criticism to avoid the regime's iron fist.

---

[4] Libya became a monarchy ruled by King Idris the first. The monarchy was soon ended in 1969 by Qaddafi's coup.
[5] Ghazi Gheblawi, "Libyan Literature: The Impact of Revolution," *Minerva*, September, 2011, http://www.minervanett.no/the-impact-of-revolution/

The 2011 Uprising and Freedom of Writing

Following the footsteps of Tunisia and Egypt, Libyans marched in the streets demanding the end of the four-decade of dictatorship in February 2011. The uprising gave Libyans, especially journalists and activists the drive and the courage to finally express their thoughts freely. Hundreds and hundreds of news reports and columns in local newspapers and on news websites were published throughout the days of the revolution. The free words of the writers marched alongside with the protestors in the call for freedom and democracy.

There is no doubt that works of literature give a deep insight of a country's spirit. Poets and fiction writers also had a great share in reflecting the people's thirst for freedom. Massive amounts of literary works, especially poems, were produced in all sorts of forums- newspapers, radio and TV, social media, and literary festivals. Other works, such as novels, were revived and translated due to their ban by Qaddafi; works like *In The Country of Men* by Hisham Matar[6] opened a gate to readers from the globe to have a better understanding of the Libyan society and its long- term suffering of oppression. Short stories were also published throughout the uprising especially during the early months of the revolution. Libyan authors published their works mostly in local newspapers and on the author's' websites or social media pages, such as Facebook.

The involvement of Libyan writers in the uprising was great and even preceded the call for the revolution in 2011. They played an important role in channeling the truth to the international world and contributed greatly in making the change possible. Their pledge to the Libyan people put them in constant risk with the regime; their writings during the early months of the revolution had heavy revolutionary sentiments. Writers like Azza Al-Maghour described the fights and the bloody battles of the young and the old against the oppressed regime.

The Cultural Meanings of Colors

Colors in almost any language and culture have great connotative meanings that indicate specific cultural concepts. They convey different messages to people of different cultures and traditions "The connotation of the colors is not only an important tool for intercultural communication, but also an important cultural and prominent component of the relationship between the cultural content, cultural form, between the interdependence and interaction."[7]

Every language has a set of basic color terms and these sets of colors can symbolize cultural codes that differ from one language to the other.

---

[6] Hisham Matar, *In The Country of Men,* (Viking Press, 2006), and was nominated for the 2006 Man Booker Prize and the Guardian First Book Award.

[7] Guimei He, "English and Chinese Cultural Connotation of Color Words in Comparison," in *Asian Social Science,* 5(7) (2009), 160.

Understanding the specific connotations of colors helps to effect smooth communication. The literature on colors and their connotative meanings strongly stresses their importance in understanding societies. For example, the color "red" in China has a positive meaning; it represents joy and happiness. "It is the color of good luck and is used for decoration and wedding dressing"[8]. The same color stands for violence and anger in Europe and North America and blood and fire in the Arab world.

The colors black and white, according to Xing[9] and Hassan, Al-Sammerai and Bin Abdul Kadir[10], are the most contrastive and easily identified, even in Arab culture. White is considered a positive color that connotes peace and purity. Black symbolizes the opposite; it connotes darkness, pessimism, and death. Red, as already shown, is positive, but can also have negative connotations. Al-Adaileh[11] notes that its negative connotations seem to be more common than the positive ones. Red, for example, is associated with blood and fire; hence, it connotes anger and danger. The color yellow can also represent positive and negative meanings. For example, in Jordanian Arabic, yellow mostly indicates fear and disease. When people are frightened, their faces may turn yellow and when they get sick, they may become pale and yellowish. However, yellow is also associated with the sun and, therefore, connotes brightness and light. Green according to Hassan, Al-Sammerai and Bin Abdul Kadir[12] is a traditional color of Islam due to its association with nature. In the Qur`an, believers of Allah are promised that they would wear fine green silk in heaven. It is clear, then, that green connotes positivity and indicates growth, harmony, and health. As for the color blue, its association with the sea and clear sky connotes highly positive values such as calmness and clearness in the Arab world, on the other hand, it represents cold and evil in East Asia, whereas in the Netherlands, it represents warmth.

As discussed above, colors represent cultural codes that can connote either positive or negative concepts in a language, thus, it is no surprise to see such cultural codes functioning in literary texts to help convey certain messages in context. The following section discusses briefly the use of colors as connotative codes in Libyan short stories.

---

[8] Ibid.

[9] Janet Xing, "Semantics and Pragmatics of Color Terms in Chinese," in *Studies of Chinese Linguistics: Functional Approaches* (Hong Kong: Western Washington University, 2008).

[10] Amna Hassan, Nabiha Al-Sammerai and Fakhrul Bin Abdul Kadir, "How Colours are Semantically Construct in the Arabic and English Culture: A Comparative Study," in *English Language Teaching* 4 (3) (2011), p. 206-213.

[11] Bilal Al-Adaileh, "The Connotations of Arabic Colour Terms, " in *Linguistica Online* (Jordan, Al-Hussein Bin Talal University, 2012).

[12] op.cit Amna Hassan, Nabiha Al-Sammerai and Fakhrul Bin Abdul Kadir, p.206-213

Colors in Libyan Short Stories: A Previous Study

As mentioned earlier in the introduction, Qaddafi`s regime forced censorship on Libyan writers throughout his four decade rule. Starting from the 1980`s, the freedom of literary writing decreased due to the many arrests of authors and young educators. Qaddafi`s regime monitored literary works that contained any criticism, and locked up several successful writers, such as AbdulSalam Shehab who later quit writing, and Gum`ah Bukleib who returned to writing after 20 years in prison. In the 1990`s, short- story writers had limited freedom and less public opinion. At that time, writers such as Ahmed Aghila and Salem Al-Abbar avoided writing about the political, economic, and social facts in the society and turned to creative works that reflected hopes and fantasies. Libyan authors relied a lot on both poetry and short stories because they felt that longer works, such as novels, needed to be based on a society with a more solid structure and stronger industrial and economical features that form a country's identity, an identity that Libyan authors and people, perhaps, had lost touch with.

The volume of poetry and short stories produced in that era is large, however, there is, unfortunately, very little scholarly work on Libyan short stories specifically on a linguistic level. A stylistics analysis study by Elnaili[13] analyzed the effect of colors to connote and represent positive and negative images in Libyan short stories before the Arab Spring. With the censorship, Libyan writers and creative writing authors found the need to express their thoughts and socio-political criticism implicitly in order to avoid imprisonment and even execution. They adopted a language style to serve their literary work in transmitting their messages to their audience. One of these styles is the use of colors in showcasing positive and negative representations in the society. The study observed a linguistic pattern Libyan writers use as a technique to channel their criticism and messages to the readers. They lean heavily on colors to mostly connote cultural signs and meanings. They employ colors in empowering and disempowering characters that represent concepts and ideologies in Libyan society. They are also used to create positive and negative moods that help romanticize and dramatize events and atmospheres in the story. The color black is commonly used to intensify negative images and create dramatic moods. This is seen in the way Libyan authors like Saleh Saad Younis associate the color black with religious figures` visions of the villages to control people's` fate: *black rain drops*, *black flood*, and the *black tears*, and Ahmed Al-Fagih: *black* sky to predict darkness and obscurity. The color white on the other hand is mostly used to create positive images and sometimes to romanticize characters. The most noticeable usage of

---

[13] Elnaili, Safa. "*Adjectives of Colour in Libyan Short Stories: A Stylistic Analysis.*" In *Language, Literature and Style in Africa,* Edited by Arua E. Arua, Taiwo Abioye, & Kehinde A. Ayoola ,p. 131-141. Cambridge Scholars Publishing. 2014.

white was seen in describing religious figures` beards as white beards. Being a color that symbolizes peace and clarity, the white beard helps portray the religious men as flawless and peaceful, thus empowering them.

Other colors in the story such as: yellow, red, blue, and green varied in their usages. Yellow, like white, was used to paint positive images of the rock in *The Yellow Rock* as being a flammable source of light and by that connoting hope. Similar is its use for beautiful fertile fields in *The Locusts* as Fagih describes a pretty image of the yellow barley fields in the village. Green is also used to picture similar positive images of nature in The Locusts where we see images of green trees and a green village to pose a happy mood in the story that reflects the victorious atmosphere in the village after collecting the locusts. Colors red and blue, however, were employed for both positive and negative images. Red was part of the Sheikh`s[14] pessimistic vision in *The Yellow Rock* as he describes the sky as red in indication of blood and fire, whereas in *The Locusts* the color was used to romanticize the view in the village where we see red horizon to indicate sunrise, which in turn connotes a new hopeful day. The blue sky in *The Sultan`s Flotilla* by Sadiq Nayhoum contributed along with white in describing a positive image of the sailing ships, but in *The Locusts* the color had a different effect: The villagers` blue veins connoted their anger and frustration of the coming disaster, therefore, creating an atmosphere of despair in the story.

Azza Al-Maghour: Selected Short Stories

Azza Al-Maghour is a Libyan senior lawyer who graduated from law school in Benghazi and pursued her studies in Paris, France. She was a member of the inaugural committee in the Tripoli Bar Association that issued in 1998 the first Libyan human rights report. Al-Maghour also assisted a Libyan detained in Guantanamo as the family's lawyer. She was the first to address and lecture about the HIV infected citizens in Benghazi. She addressed domestic issues such as family abuse, women's rights, and sexual harassment. She is a lawyer, a human rights activist and an author.

Al-Maghour's name is well recognized in modern Arabic fiction. She has two collections of short stories: *Thirty Stories of My City* (2013) with Dar Al Rowad Press in Tripoli, and *Fashloum* (2012). A number of her stories have been translated into English, like *The Bicycle*. She has a large volume of short stories published online[15]. With the Libyan uprising, Al-Maghour's attention has been turned to nonfiction writing; she published several political articles and essays discussing the country struggle for freedom.

---

[14] Old man/religious man.
[15] All short stories selected for this study are available online magazine in Libya Al-Mustakbal: http://www.libya-al-mostakbal.org/

For this paper, I have selected a number of seven short stories that were all published in 2011 on Libya Al Mostakbal website. I have selected these particular stories based on their revolutionary theme; all seven of them narrate stories during the uprising in 2011. In these narratives Al-Maghour tells the stories of people breaking their silence and resisting oppression, she also pictures actual scenes and portrays real stories to the reader that happened that year. The short stories are the following: Fatima (May 25th 2011)[16], Oh My Lord (June 6th 2011)[17], Fashloom (June 9th 2011)[18], Yadj (June 25th 2011)[19] (footnote), Jellyfish (July 21st 2011),[20] Olive Tree (July 25th 2011)[21], and Azzawia`s Spring[22] (August 20th 2011).

Resistance and Empowerment: *Black* vs. *White*

The colors black and white are considered culturally contrast and connote opposite meanings in Arabic. Black represents darkness, pessimism, death, disease, mourning, etc.; it is always associated in Arabic language with bad thoughts and emotions and is used to picture negative things. For instance, if someone were in fierce with his/her bad luck, the expression would be: *black day*, or if someone were to describe an evil person he/she would describe him/her as person with a *black heart*. Egyptians, for example, when mourning the death of their beloved ones wear black. Most Arabic societies believe seeing a black cat could be a bad sign or something horrible is about to happen. The color white on the other hand symbolizes positive meanings; wearing white is usually related to happy events such as the bride`s white dress in a wedding, the pilgrims` white clothes in their pilgrimage to Mecca, in Islam the deceased, especially those who died martyrs in war, are wrapped in white sheets to express joy for their honorable departure, white also symbolizes peace, and if someone was to be described as good hearted the expression would be: white heart.

---

[16] Almaghour, Azza (Libya Al-Mustakbal). "Fatima." May, 2011.
http://www.libya-al-mostakbal.org/news/clicked/9003
[17] Almaghour, Azza (Libya Al-Mustakbal). "Oh My Lord." June, 2011.
http://www.libya-al-mostakbal.org/news/clicked/9563
[18] Almaghour, Azza (Libya Al-Mustakbal). "Fashloum." June, 2011.
http://www.libya-al-mostakbal.org/news/clicked/9781
[19] Almaghour, Azza (Libya Al-Mustakbal). "Yadj." June, 2011.
http://www.libya-al-mostakbal.org/news/clicked/10443
[20] lmaghour, Azza (Libya Al-Mustakbal). "Jellyfish." July, 2011.
http://www.libya-al-mostakbal.org/news/clicked/11326
[21] Almaghour, Azza (Libya Al-Mustakbal). "Olive Tree." July, 2011.
http://www.libya-al-mostakbal.org/news/clicked/11843
[22] Almaghour, Azza (Libya Al-Mustakbal). "Azzawia`s Spring." August, 2011.
http://www.libya-al-mostakbal.org/news/clicked/12377
Azzawia is a Libyan city located 45 kilometers west Tripoli.

According to Elnaili`s[23] study, writers in Libyan short stories heavily used these two opposite colors to indicate power and weakness. The color white was mentioned several times to describe the religious figures` beards as white to connote wisdom and experience, whereas the color black was used to describe the people's` fortune and future: *black sky* & *black rain* drops. With these associations, the authors are revealing to the reader, indirectly, that the public or the layman is always disempowered while the political and/or the religious man is superior and in power.

Azza Al-Maghour re-empowers the people by describing their clothes, their appearances, and their lands and flowers with white. In *The Olive Tree* she describes how Sheikh Mohammed takes off his military suit and wears his white pants and jilbab, which is the traditional Libyan clothing for men, when leaving his house for protest to represent rebellion against the military rule and the fight against Qaddafi with his true Libyan self. In the same story she describes how the city of Zintan rises against oppression and lights up like "a white candle". In *Yadj* we see Ahmed, who just returned from a protest to deliver to his wife the death of their son, described as tall and with a white beard to show tolerance and that the fight for freedom knows no age. His wife watches her martyred child covered in a white sheet, the family farewells their beloved one and celebrates his martyrdom. In *Jellyfish* Qaddafi`s troops carry white flags to trick the protesters into making them believe that they are calling for peace, and as they mix with the crowed who lend their trust to them, they open fire on the protestors. In stories pre-the Arab Spring, white was a property only those close to the regime and highly seated in the pyramid owned, however, Al-Maghour associates white with Qaddafi`s soldiers, not to empower or glorify their image, but rather to reveal the true color of the deceived regime and how *white* was used to camouflage their darkness.

As for the color black, Al-Maghour strongly employs it to represent the tyranny and injustice of the dictatorship. She describes Qaddafi`s men in *Jellyfish* as octopuses that hide in the deep sea in rocks, strangle their prey and pull them down into the deep; she summarizes the regime in her last line of the story: "... the octopus is a cowered... it lives in the deep of the sea and prefers the dark, escapes once a swimmer approaches it and shoots its *black* ink". The color black is also used to describe the regime's weapons and assaults against civilians; in *Fatima* the author paints the image of the aftermath of the explosions and shelling houses of the rebels where the smoke is black and covers the sky like a *black* hovering cloud that seeps into your chest and chocks you to death.

---

[23] Elnaili, Safa. "*Adjectives of Colour in Libyan Short Stories: A Stylistic Analysis.*" In *Language, Literature and Style in Africa,* Edited by Arua E. Arua, Taiwo Abioye, & Kehinde A. Ayoola, p.131-141. Cambridge Scholars Publishing. 2014.

Stripping Qaddafi` off his *Green*

In Arabic culture green is considered a positive color; this is probably due to its association with the description of paradise in the Qur`an where people will be wearing green garments of fine silk. It is also the color of nature and plants and thus represents prosperity and growth. In most Arabic countries, when seeing a garden, green grass, or plants in a dream, it is considered an optimistic sign.

Before the downfall of Qaddafi, green was mainly a color that most Libyans feared. Green was the color of the Libyan flag: buildings and schools where all painted in white and green, gates of almost all governmental buildings must be painted green to show loyalty to the regime. Every year on the anniversary of Qaddafi`s Al-Fateh revolution[24] green flags and lights were used to decorate the cities` streets and squares. Whoever wore green was immediately considered a follower and a loyalist to Qaddafi. Some people even avoided using the color green in a negative context in public in fear of punishment. In literary works, writers avoided the use of green in any political sense.

In Al-Maghour`s *Olive Trees* we see liberation from the political symbolism of the color and its connection with the regime: Sheikh Mohammed "... takes off his *green* military suite and makes an oath not to wear it again, ever". This indicates freedom of political oppression and breaking out of the Qaddafi`s 42 years cycle of dictatorship. In *Azzawia`s Spring*, she brings out the conflict between the people and the regime through the use of the color; early in the story she pictures how spring came early to the city of Azzawia and how the lands and fields turned green in indication to the Arab Spring, then later in the story Qaddafi`s soldiers storm into the city with force and occupy its main square with their tanks and armory and "... hanged the *green* rags on its buildings". In *Oh My Lord*, death of the unarmed civilians is pictured and located next to the *green* gates: "a scream exploded in the middle of the gathered crowd in front of the green iron gate of Tariq Bin Ziyad school where someone was hitting his head in mourn and shouting 'they killed him...they killed him'". The text reveals the ugliness of the regime here by the use of the color green as the cause of violence.

Red is Pride

As mentioned earlier, and unlike in China, red in Arabic cultures has a negative connotation that stands for blood, war, fire, destruction, and anger; For example, seeing red in dreams or visions is considered pessimistic.

Although the color red, compared to other colors such as white and black, is not heavily used in the literary works produced before the revolution, however,

---

[24] Qaddafi called his coup in 1969 Al-Fateh (Victory) revolution.

the few contexts where it was placed has a negative image. One example can be seen in *The Yellow Rock* where the Fagih[25] describes to the villagers his vision of the people's future; he pictures it with *black raindrops* and *red skies* to create fear in them and thus fear him.

Azza Al-Maghour continues to employ the color the same way, however, she contextualizes it to draw a picture of the Libyans' fight for freedom. In her stories, red paints bloody scenes of citizens falling dead in battle against the regime's unmerciful soldiers; In *Jellyfish* we see Qaddafi's regime occupying Tagoora's[26] beautiful white sand beaches and builds military bases with giant iron gates painted in white and *red*, and Qaddafi's men wearing *red hats* and green suits marching towards the protesters to break them up. We see violent scenes of blood on the streets in *Oh My Lord* where a young boy from Benghazi lies dead after a soldier shot him. Al-Maghour, and despite of the negative connotation of the color, uses it in a manner of pride for the Libyans' war for freedom; In *Fatima*, a young girl gets an injury in her right foot after her home was shelled, *dark red blood* is described running out of her wound, but she survived her wound and "held her father's hand tightly, leaned on him and started walking". Probably the most challenging context to the regime is found in *Fashloom*: "With sunrise the traces of last night can be seen along the main street, the rocks, the burned tires, and the echoes that are still stuck in the air, and the writings on the walls with *red* ... 'Libya's free...the unjust is out'". Al-Maghour vividly shows in her narrative how the Libyan people are unafraid of spilling their blood in the name of freedom.

Green, Red, and Black: Libya's Independence

Despite of the color green's association to Qaddafi's regime, the color red's representation of blood and violence, and the color black's negative and pessimistic relevance, Libyans fought their oppressor with these three colors; the colors of Libya's independence flag in 1951. They retrieved the beauty of their green mountains, they were proud of the sacrifices of their forefathers and themselves for freedom and stability, and they feared not the darkness of uncertainty[27].

Conclusion

Azza Al-Maghour gives an example of how writing, even a short story, can

---

[25] Fagih, Ahmed. *The Libyan Short Story: A Research and Anthology.* United States: Xlibiris Corporation, 2008.

[26] Op. Cit. Almaghour, Azza, Libya Al-Mustakbal July 2011

[27] Red in the Libyan flag symbolizes the blood Libyans spilled for independence from the Italians, black was the Senussi movement (who led the fight to independence) flag color, and black stands for the green mountains of Libya.

be revolutionary in itself. Her use of colors to explicitly describe socio-political change shows resistance to language style of literary works under Qaddafi's dogmatic rule. Libyans are finally empowered and presented in a positive way whereas figures of the regime are given negative images. With implementing colors in her literary contexts she criticizes the regime explicitly and more directly. For example, *white*, the color of optimism and peace is no longer a property of religious and/or political personals; it is the symbol of the Libyan citizen, the rebel and the hero of her stories.

Journal of South Asian and Middle Eastern Studies Vol. XL, No.2, WINTER 2017

A Stage for the Revolution: Muharram and the Paradigm of Karbala in the context of Khomeini's Struggle with the Shah

Javier Gil Guerrero*

Introduction

An important part of Iran's Islamic revolution was the role that religious rituals and Persian folklore played in the social upheaval. Khomeini successfully conjured the spirits of the past in order to bring change to the present. This paper describes how Khomeini made use of (and reinterpreted) the slaughter at Karbala (680) in order to mobilize the population. Throughout this process Khomeini not only helped to revive old traditions, but he also reactivated old concepts like "martyrdom" while instilling new meaning to them.[1]

The objective of this paper is to put the Khomeini's use of Muharram (the commemoration of Hussein's death at Karbala) in perspective and examine the nuances that he added to the story and the rituals that had emanated from it. Through the use of Muharram, Khomeini "presented the revolutionary movement against the regime as a morality play […] where heroes and villains could be easily identified."[2] The study locates Khomeini's refashioning of Karbala within the context of the Iranian revolution and the Pahlavi state, including the struggle for the ideological orientation of Shia Islam, the attempts to monopolize the Karbala commemorations by the Iranian authorities and the repeated use of those ceremonies for political motivations.

The contention of this study is that through his approach to the story of

---

*Javier Gil Guerrero is a professor of Middle Eastern History at the Universidad Francisco de Vitoria. He has recently published a book on the Iranian revolution, *The Carter Administration & the Fall of Iran's Pahlavi Dynasty* (Palgrave Macmillan, 2016) as well as several papers on Iran and the Persian Gulf in the *British Journal of Middle Eastern Studies* and the *Instituto Español de Estudios Estratégicos*. He regularly writes on Islam in the Spanish press.

[1] Elisabeth Jane Yarbakhsha, "Green martyrdom and the Iranian state," *Continuum: Journal of Media & Cultural Studies*, Volume 28, Issue 1, 2014.

[2] Jahangir Amuzegar, *The Dynamics of the Iranian Revolution: The Pahlavi's Triumph and Tragedy* (New York: State University of New York Press, 1991), 31.

Hussein, Khomeini transformed the traditional image of the Imam from a passive and abused victim of injustice to a revolutionary martyr who fought to death against tyranny and oppression. Hussein became the prototype of a permanent revolutionary in a particular "Liberation Theology" of Islam.[3] Khomeini's innovative portrayal of Hussein reinterpreted one of the cultural pillars of Shia Islam in order to advance an "activist" approach to religion instead of the "quietist" one. The Karbala commemorations were thus dressed to fit a message of confrontation against the Shah in which the revolution was the only possible way for Shiites irrespective of its chances of success.

The core of this paper is the description of Khomeini's use of Muharram during his two clashes with the regime of the Shah in 1963 and 1978. The account is preceded by a brief overview of the historical events that inspired the mourning rituals of Muharram and their significance in Iranian culture and history. The aim is to contextualize the shifting interpretation of the ceremonies in the 1960s and 1970s through the particular beliefs and customs of Persian folklore and Shia Islam.

Hussein, Karbala and Muharram

The commemorations of Muharram revolve around the tragic end of Imam Hussein's life in the year 680. Grandson of the Prophet Muhammad and son of the first Shia imam (and fourth Sunni Caliph), Ali. The slaughter of Hussein and the division concerning Prophet Muhammad's rightful heirs constitutes the epicentre of the divisions between Shia and Sunni Muslims. The Shiites believe that the Prophet's cousin and son-in-law Ali had been designated leader of the Muslim community by the Prophet himself on his deathbed. It was a designation of divine inspiration, not a personal choice: Ali had been named heir to Muhammad's leadership by God. The Sunnis, on the other hand, ignored Ali's claim (accusing him of falsifying the story) and proceeded to accept the ruling of the elders of Medina, who selected Abu Bakr as the new head of the community. For Abu Bakr and the Sunnis, Muhammad had died without issuing any specific instruction regarding succession to his position. The Shiites (followers of Ali) then emerged as a faction disputing Abu Bakr's position. Ali's claim was again ignored when Abu Bakr died and Umar became the new Caliph. He was again sidestepped when Umar was succeeded by Uthman. Yet, after the assassination of Uthman in 656 Ali was finally chosen as the fourth Caliph, briefly uniting the Muslims under his leadership. But Ali's rule was a tumultuous one, when several governors of the provinces appointed by Osman refused to accept Ali as the new Caliph. One of them, Muawiya, governor of Syria, openly rebelled

---

[3] Hamid Dabashi, *Islamic Liberation Theology: Resisting the Empire* (New York: Routledge, 2008), 188.

against him. Muawiya, a late convert to Islam of the Umayyad family, blamed Ali for Uthman's assassination.

After a bloody military campaign in today's Iraq, Ali was assassinated in Kufa. While the Shiites maintained that Ali's son Hassan was his rightful successor, Muawiya became Caliph. Instead of pursuing the violent struggle between Sunnis and Shiites, Hassan reached an agreement with Muawiya in 670 and accepted to forego his claim and retired from politics to live a peaceful life in Medina away from the power intrigues. But when he died and the claim to the Imamate passed to his brother Hussein, the confrontation was revived. Unlike his older brother, Hussein had no intention to compromise on his right to leadership of the Muslim community. He decided to fight to defend his divine appointment as Imam and battled Muawiya's son, Caliph Yazid. In his way to Kufa from Medina, Imam Hussein and his companions were surrounded by Yazid's army on the west bank of the Euphrates River, in the plain of Karbala.

It was the first day of the month of Muharram in the Islamic year of 680. While Yazid's army numbered several thousands, Hussein commanded only a few hundred (some of them women and children). Outnumbered and besieged, after several days that alternated between skirmishes and infructuous negotiations, Hussein's camp was finally overrun on the tenth day of Muharram. Hussein and 72 companions were massacred while the rest were taken prisoner and enslaved.

The "battle" of Karbala and Hussein's martyrdom sealed the enmity and distrust that would mark the relations between Sunnis and Shiites. The Karbala tragedy represents the culmination in the gradual rupture of the Muslim community that followed the death of Prophet Muhammad. Those first ten days of Muharram became in time one of the most important dates in the Shia calendar. A yearly period of remembrance and ritual re-enactments that cements the identity of Shiites.

The mourning of Muharram and the rituals that those sacred days entailed constituted a determination by the Shiites to never forget the crime of Karbala. While the period of mourning begins the first day of Muharram, it culminates in the ninth day, called Tassua and the tenth day, called Ashura.

The events of Ashura take place at two levels: in *Alam al-mithal* (the World of the Archetypal Images), and *Alam al-khayal* (the World of the Imagination).[4] The ceremonies help the faithful to establish a bridge between the two. Muharram is also a memory of the future, of the promised Mahdi, the Shia messiah, the Twelfth Imam who went into occultation. For Twelver Shia Islam Muharram also serves to remind believers of the incoming redemption through the arrival of the hidden Imam that will outdo all the wrongdoing suffered by the Shiites.

---

[4] William C. Chittick, *The Sufi Path of Knowledge: Ibn al-'Arabi's Metaphysics of Imagination* (Albany, N.Y.: State University of New York Press, 1989), 117.

Thus, the Ashura ceremonies bridge past, present and future in an eschatological narrative of treachery, death and redemption.

The month of Muharram serves to commemorate the tragedy at Karbala through sermons, passion plays, demonstrations, poetry and mourning.

Rauza Khawani is a dramatic recitation of excerpts of the book *The Garden of Martyrs*, which narrates the life and death of Hussein and other Shia martyrs. It takes place in closed environments, like mosques, in black tents erected in public squares or private houses. It is a social gathering of neighbours, friends and relatives. Men and women listen to the recitations in different rooms. The interiors are specially decorated for the occasion with black flags and replica weapons from the time of Hussein's martyrdom. "A unity of feeling of great intensity" is aroused in the attendees by the passionate narration of the events and the singing of songs that commemorate them. They end identifying with the suffering of the martyrs and lamenting and grieving the fate of Ali, Hussein and other saints.[5]

Sinehzani is a male funeral procession of self-flagellation (called *Tatbir* when one hits himself with a sword or a stick) and breast-beating. The participants, dressed in black, march through the streets chanting elegies while following a black coffin representing the martyred Imam Hussein's body.[6]

Perhaps one of the most interesting rites is the *Tazieh* passion play, "a communal act of collective redemption."[7] It resembles the Catholic processions that take place during the last week of Lent before Easter. Tazieh is a theatrical representation of the Karbala events orchestrated to keep passions running high throughout the duration of the performance with a bloody and melodramatic retelling of the suffering of Hussein and his family.[8] Although every detail of the stage play is well known by those watching, the depiction of the slaughter at Karbala never fails to excite the most intense emotions of the public. Tazieh is a theatre of condolence that serves as a catalyst of all the variations on the thematic mourning of Hussein.[9]

The diverse *matams* (passionate acts of lamentation) function as a tool to strengthen the bonds between Shiites while deepening their cultural identity. A month in which tears mingled with blood in a frenzy of weeping and wailing. Through, atonement, penance and mourning the individual looks upon himself

---

[5] Peter Chelkowski, "Popular Entertainment, Media and Social Change in Twentieth-Century Iran," in Peter Avery, Gavin Hambly and Charles Melville (eds.), *The Cambridge History of Iran. From Nadir Shah to the Islamic Republic, vol. 7* (Cambridge: Cambridge University Press, 1991), 771.

[6] Janet Afary and Kevin B. Anderson, *Foucault and the Iranian Revolution: Gender and the Seductions of Islamism* (Chicago: Chicago University Press, 2005), 44.

[7] Hamid Dabashi, *Islamic Liberation Theology*, 187.

[8] Janet Afary and Kevin B. Anderson, *Foucault and the Iranian Revolution*, 44-46.

[9] Hamid Dabashi, *Islamic Liberation Theology*, 187.

through the mirror of Hussein. An act of public confession in which they bear witness to the martyrdom of Hussein and at the same time atone for the guilt of their sins.[10] The matams constitute a key part of the cultural and political heritage of Iranians.[11] As Jalal Toufic has stated, Muharram is "a memory that is torture. […] torture that had to be inflicted on humans in order for them to be able to remember."[12] In this case, a remembrance of what it means to be a Shiite.

Although some scholars have pointed out that some of the ceremonies that take place during Muharram, have pre-Islamic origins and while some ulama have condemned the rituals, tradition holds that it was Hussein's captive sister Zeinab who began the Muharram mourning tradition by making speeches on the tragedy of Karbala in order to keep the memory of her brother alive.[13]

Tazieh received a boost when the Safavids embraced Shia Islam and made it the state religion of Persia. Tazieh and other ceremonies became an indispensable tool for propagating Shia Islam among their subjects. As the Muharram celebrations were encouraged by the monarchs, the mourning period became a patriotic and nationalistic issue as well as a religious one.[14]

Unlike the Safavids and the Qajars, the Pahlavis resented the rituals associated with Muharram. Considering them a fanatical tradition and an obstacle to his ambitions to modernize and westernize Iran, Reza Shah discouraged and restricted some aspects of the religious ceremonies of Muharram.[15] Finally, in 1932 he banned Tazieh and other ceremonies.[16] He also demolished the famous Takia-e Dawlat, built in Tehran in the 1860s by a late Qajar monarch, Nasser al-Din Shah, to host sumptuous representations of Tazieh.

For Reza Shah, Muharram paved the way for "barbaric acts of mass exaltation" that had no place in a modern country.[17] Because of his policies the tradition decayed. Yet, they experienced a gradual resurgence after his abdication in 1941. His son, Mohammad Reza Pahlavi, partially lifted the ban. Tazieh became a subject of scholarly research in the sixties and the focus of some representations in the Pahlavi-sponsored Shiraz Arts Festival.[18] Empress Farah attended one

---

[10] Janet Afary and Kevin B. Anderson, *Foucault and the Iranian Revolution*, 53-54.

[11] See Peter J. Chelkowski, *Ta'ziyeh: Ritual and Drama in Iran* (New York: New York University Press, 1979)

[12] Jalal Toufic, *'Ashura': This Blood Spilled in My Veins* (Forthcoming Books, 2005), 9.

[13] Jalal Toufic, 'Ashura', 14.

[14] Jamshid Malekpur, *The Islamic Drama* (London: Frank Cass, 2005), 13.

[15] Willem M. Floor, *The History of Theater in Iran* (Mage Publishers, 2005), 197.

[16] Nevertheless, the decree was never enforced in its entirety in certain rural areas.

[17] Don Rubin, Chua Soo Pong, Ravi Chaturvedi, Ramendu Majumdar, Minoru Tanokura and Katharine Brisane (eds.), *The World Encyclopedia of Contemporary Theatre: Asia/Pacific* (New York: Routledge, 2001), 195.

[18] Gholam Reza Afkhami, *The Life and Times of the Shah* (Berkeley: university of California Press, 2009), 417.

of the performances, which were viewed by tens of thousands of Iranians.[19] The official representations of Tazieh also served a political purpose: the Shah wanted to discourage the private and local performances (prone to politicization) organized by mosques and neighbourhood associations and favour instead lavish government-sponsored plays with no political subtext.[20]

But Tazieh had survived on a local level and emerged in full force in the mid-seventies. It suddenly became an act of indigenous self-reaffirmation in confrontation with the modern ways of entertaining that had come from the West (radio, cinema, modern music). Tazieh was rediscovered by new generations as a way to reconnect with their roots and as an alternative to (hollow and degenerate) Western means of entertaining that constituted a sort of cultural imperialism. Against the Pahlavis infatuation with the cultural products of Europe and America, Tazieh became a symbol of indigenous traditions and forms of expression.

Khomeini's interpretation and use of Muharram

Before Khomeini decided to make use of the Muharram rituals and Tazieh, those events had already been manipulated throughout history by Iranian rulers. Prior to Khomeini, the commemorations of Muharram had also included veiled political commentary. Yet, Reza Shah's opposition to them tainted the reputation of the Pahlavis regarding Muharram and made it easier for Khomeini to use them to rally the population against the Shah. Although the power struggle between the clergy and the government in Iran is an historical pattern, the way Khomeini used the figures of Yazid and Hussein in order to galvanize the population was a novelty. He skilfully reinterpreted Shia mythology and projected it to the present.

Traditionally, the Tazieh favoured by the Safavids and the Qajars was a passive performance In the portrayal of Hussein, his virtuosity went hand to hand with his resignation to a doomed fate.[21] Hussein appeared as a lamb in the slaughterhouse, quietly accepting his fate. It was mainly an act of *Mazlumiyyat*, ("having been wronged") and he was *Hussein-e Mazlum*, ("Hussein who was wronged").[22] The meaning of Muharram was to avoid Hussein's second death: he had been already martyred but his memory could not be allowed to fade away from the world of the living.

For Khomeini, remembrance was not enough. It was useless if it was not followed by a substantial transformation of those who participated in the events

---

[19] Don Rubin, Chua Soo Pong, Ravi Chaturvedi, Ramendu Majumdar, Minoru Tanokura and Katharine Brisane (eds.), *The World Encyclopedia of Contemporary Theatre*, 195.

[20] Janet Afary and Kevin B. Anderson, *Foucault and the Iranian Revolution*, 46.

[21] See Ibrahim Moussawi, *Shi'ism & the Democratisation Process in Iran* (London: SAQI, 2011).

[22] Hamid Dabashi, *Islamic Liberation Theology*, 187.

of Muharram. Like the case of the Roman Catholic passion plays, the Tazieh was open to many different interpretations. Khomeini took advantage of that and presented a militant and belligerent reinterpretation of Karbala that no longer stressed the innocent nature of Hussein as a passive victim. Unlike the Christian passion plays, Khomeini stressed the militant nature of Hussein and his readiness to fight and die for true Islam and justice.[23] Hussein was no Christ on the cross, but a "Master of Martyrs", an actual fighter against tyranny.[24]

This intellectual framework was not only the product of Khomeini. It was developed in the sixties and the seventies by other influential intellectuals and clergymen like Ali Shariati (who was despised by many conservative clergymen, and was a decisive influence on Khomeini and the revolution), Morteza Motahari and Ayatollah Taleqani.[25]

Ali Shariati was the thinker behind the idea of active martyrdom. He protected the view that when Muslims faced a powerful foe they could choose between two options: 1, a quietist approach that allowed oppression to continue; 2, an activist approach to martyrdom in order to pave the way for others to live as true Muslims. Martyrdom was thus reinterpreted as a sacrifice for mankind. Following this rationale, Shariati explained that when Imam Hussein became aware of the military defeat against the forces of Yazid he chose death knowing that he could achieve more with his martyrdom than by living. His example would curse his enemies and set an example for the future generations of Shiites. "It is in this way that the dying of a human being guarantees the life of a nation." Martyrdom was an invitation to the faithful, a message that if someone could not prevail in his fight against oppression the only remaining option was death.[26]

Aside from the reinterpretation of Hussein's death, Khomeini used the events of Karbala as a metaphor of his struggle against the Shah. Because the story was well known by all Iranians, the presentation of the conflict between Yazid and Hussein within the conceptual framework of a struggle between Islam and injustice against tyranny and disbelief was a convenient way to influence the population with his revolutionary message.[27]

In the Tazieh, almost equally important is the figure of Yazid. If Hussein is the embodiment of bravery, faithfulness, humbleness and loyalty; Yazid is the representation of wickedness, tyranny, disbelief and treason. While Khomeini never compared himself to Hussein, he repeatedly presented the Shah as *Yazid-e*

---

[23] Janet Afary and Kevin B. Anderson, *Foucault and the Iranian Revolution*, 64.

[24] L.A. Reda, "Khatt-e Imam: The Followers of Khomeini's Line," in Arshin Adib-Moghaddam (ed.), *A Critical Introduction to Khomeini* (Cambridge: Cambridge University Press, 2014), 125.

[25] Ingvild Flaskerud, "Redemptive Memories: Portraiture in the Cult of Commemoration" in Pedram Khosronejad, *Unburied Memories*, 25.

[26] Janet Afary and Kevin B. Anderson, *Foucault and the Iranian Revolution*, 62-63.

[27] Hatam Qaderi, "Thoughts and Faces behind the Islamic Revolution," in Saeid Edalat Nezhad and Hossein Aghazed (eds.), *The Islamic Revolution of Iran*, 112.

Zaman ("the Yazid of the age").[28] Comparing the Shah to Yazid was to compare the Shah with the most hated historical figure among Shiites.

"It is now the afternoon of Ashura," said Khomeini in the summer of 1977, "Sometimes when I recall the events of Ashura, a question occurs to me: If the Umayyads, and the regime of Yazid, son of Muawiya, wished to make war against Hussein, why did they commit such savage and inhumane crimes against the defenceless women and innocent children?"[29] They did so, Khomeini answered, because they wanted to uproot the family of the Prophet and Islam itself. Nowadays, he continued, there was another tyrant committing horrible deeds, this time against the clergy and its own subjects. As with Yazid, the wickedness of the Shah had to do with his "fundamental opposition to Islam itself and the existence of the religious class."[30]

By making the Shah a modern-day Yazid, Khomeini made almost impossible any compromise with him. How could the opposition seek a negotiated solution to the conflict with Yazid? Any negotiation with Yazid was equal to treason and the only possible way forward was to fight. In time, Khomeini would be compared to Hussein and the demonstrators whoever killed would embody Hussein's faithful companions: the martyrs. The message of opposition to the Shah was thus articulated through the Tazieh and other commemorations into a religious struggle led by Khomeini. There was little room left in this eschatological discourse for the secular opposition, the leftists or the communists. The narrative channelled through the religious rituals and traditions not only served to rally the people against the monarchy but also elevate the stakes in the struggle while downplaying the relevance of the secular opposition.

Khomeini was aware that the discourse of Muharram and Tazieh was necessary in order to obtain the revolutionary consensus necessary to overthrow a political system. In a society polarized among ethnic and political divisions, Shia Islam was the main uniting force that kept the country together. While a sizable part of the population was suspicious of Persian nationalism, Islam appealed to a broader public. By using the religious symbols of Muharram, Khomeini could easily achieve consensual form of rallying against the Shah.[31]

The Muharram of 1963

It's not by chance that Khomeini's first confrontation with the Shah took place during Muharram. After the police raid on the Feiziyeh theological school that

---

[28] Joanna De Groot, *Religion, Culture and Politics in Iran: From the Qajars to Khomeini* (New York: I.B. Tauris, 2007), 198.

[29] Janet Afary and Kevin B. Anderson, *Foucault and the Iranian Revolution*, 57-58.

[30] Janet Afary and Kevin B. Anderson, *Foucault and the Iranian Revolution*, 58.

[31] See Shah Alam, *Social and Political Transformation in Iran since 1979: The Role of Islam* (Delhi: Vij Books, 2015).

left several students dead and wounded, Khomeini chose the Ashura of June 2, 1963 to remind his listeners in Qom of the crimes committed by the Shah. His sermon had been carefully prepared: he linked the deaths at Feiziyeh with the impious reforms launched by the Shah with the White Revolution. He then denounced the Shah as a pawn of the United States and even called him an "infidel Jew."[32] He then compared the monarch to the treacherous Caliph Yazid.

In the days before Ashura, Khomeini had asked the seminary students in Qom to compose and recite verses and elegies on the crimes committed by the Shah and his father following the model of the narrations that were read aloud in Muharram.[33] He had also requested the clergy to establish comparisons between the crimes of Karbala and those committed by the Shah during their Ashura sermons.

Khomeini was arrested on June 5. His detention would spark a wave of protests that would culminate in the Khordad or June uprising of 1963. Although swiftly quelled, the protests left several hundred demonstrators killed. The widespread disturbances across Iran constituted the most serious challenge to the rule of the Shah since the period of Mossadeq.

As time passed, during his exile, Khomeini would frequently compare the Khordad riots to the slaughter of Karbala: "In the same manner that we mourn and beat our chests in the memory of Imam Hussein and Ashura, every year we should also mourn and beat our chests in remembrance of the 15th of Khordad."[34] Khomeini's daring statement implied that his detention and the uprising in protest for his imprisonment was an event comparable to the massacre of the Imam and his followers. He was insisting that both *tragedies* had to be remembered on equal footing.

He also attributed the Khordad uprising to the intercession of Hussein: "Do not take for granted that [the uprising of] 15 of Khordad would have occurred even if there were no mourning rituals, or mourning processions in which they beat their chests and chanted slogans. No force could have caused the 15th of Khordad to take the form it did, except for the power of the blood of the Prince of Martyrs; and no force could have [preserved] this nation, which has been subjected to attacks from all sides [...], except for these mourning rituals."[35] Like Hussein in

---

[32] Yvette Hovsepian-Bearce, *The Political Ideology of Ayatollah Khamenei* (New York: Routledge, 2016).

[33] Mohammad Hassan Rajabi, "The Role of Imam Khomeini in the Islamic Movement of Iran," in Saeid Edalat Nezhad and Hossein Aghazed (eds.), *The Islamic Revolution of Iran: A Sociological Study, vol. 1* (Tehran: Alhoda, 2001), 50.

[34] Ali Rahnema, "Ayatollah Khomeini's Rule of the Guardian Jurist: From Theory to Practice," in Arshin Adib-Moghaddam (ed.), *A Critical Introduction to Khomeini* (Cambridge: Cambridge University Press, 2014), 89.

[35] Kamran Scot Aghaie, *The Martyrs of Karbala: Shi'i Symbols and Rituals in Modern Iran* (Seattle: University of Washington Press, 2004), 78.

Karbala, Iran was besieged by enemies, but the difference was that the Shiites at Karbala could count on the leadership of Hussein, whereas Iranians in the sixties were at the mercy of the Shah, who was conspiring with Iran's enemies.

The Muharram of 1978

Religious traditions marked the tempo of the Islamic revolution in 1978: a cycle of "fortieth" was established keep the revolutionary wheel spinning. The traditional forty-day mourning period was used to stage commemorative demonstrations on the fortieth day after a bloody confrontation (in turn, those commemorative demonstrations would turn into another bloody confrontation and ignite another fortieth cycle of protest).[36]

In the last months of 1978, with the revolution already in full motion, Khomeini again decided to use to his advantage the Muslim calendar, capitalizing heavily on the sacred days of Muharram.[37] The mourning period was seen as a critical moment in the revolutionary struggle. There was concern about how the Shah would weather Ashura and avoid an outburst of violence.[38]

The Shah regarded the month of Muharram as the true test of strength in his struggle with Khomeini. At first, he planned an iron fist policy. In his conversations with British and American diplomats he said he would prevent any public religious manifestations outside the mosques. When the government announced the ban of all religious demonstrations during Muharram, even moderate clergymen like Ayatollah Shariatmadari responded by making public their intention to disobey because no believer had to seek the permission of the authorities to celebrate Muharram.[39]

The ban on the processions was viewed as the latest attempt in religious repression by the Shah. Eventually, the prohibition was deemed unfeasible and dropped. The government even agreed to change the curfew hours in Tehran to facilitate the religious celebrations.[40] The lifting of the ban showcased the impotence of the Shah and his inability to prevent the demonstrations without causing a bloodbath.[41]

Before the prohibition was lifted Khomeini reacted by insisting in sermons and urging the ulema to continue with the rituals of Muharram as an act of defiance

[36] Hamid Dabashi, *Theology of Discontent: The ideological Foundation of the Islamic Revolution in Iran* (New Brunswick: Transaction Publishers, 2006), 421.

[37] Hamid Dabashi, *Theology of Discontent*, 420.

[38] Gary Sick, *All Fall Down* (London: I.B. Tauris, 1985), 108.

[39] Jean-Charles Brotons, *US Officials and the Fall of the Shah*, 64.

[40] Ervand Abrahamian, *Iran between Two Revolutions* (Princeton: Princeton University Press, 1982), 522.

[41] Jean-Charles Brotons, *US Officials and the Fall of the Shah*, 65.

against the Shah.[42] He reminded Iranians in his speeches that Imam Hussein had taught Shiites "to overthrow tyrants." As in the times of Hussein, Islam was again in danger, a menace that required Muslims to unite and spill their blood if necessary. He welcomed the triumph of the revolution in Muharram: "There will be a great Islamic victory of freedom and justice over cruelty and treason, and an Islamic government will be proclaimed, and torrents of blood will be spilled on Ashura to mark the day of vengeance against cruelty and oppression."[43]

Khomeini came to regard the Muharram demonstrations as "a street referendum against the monarchy."[44] As in June 1963, Khomeini's speeches in December 1979 were carefully calibrated to direct tensions so that they climaxed in Ashura. [45] The religious rhetoric in the run up to Muharram reminded Iranians of their duty: "The silence of the Muslims is a betrayal of the Quran [...] Islam is an eternal tree, needs the blood of martyrs to grow."[46] As an act of defiance against the curfew, the day Muharram began, on December 2, thousands of Iranians went to the rooftops and the balconies at midnight to chant "Allahu Akbar!" Tehran was overcome by a sea of religious shouting. As a British diplomat observed, "you'd think Tehran had been transformed into a roaring ocean."[47]

On the first day of Muharram Khomeini asked soldiers to desert and join the revolutionaries framing his request in the context of a religious duty.[48] Rumours spread that Khomeini had had a dream in which he died by the sixth day of Muharram. Some mullahs asked Iranians to topple the Shah before that date so that Khomeini could die in peace.[49]

Many became convinced that the final showdown between the Shah and Khomeini would take place during Ashura. Appropriately, the demonstrations began to incorporate elements of the Tazieh in preparation for the fateful date. Many demonstrators wore symbolic black clothes (*siyapoush*) associated with remembrance and mourning. It was a mourning that mixed the loss of Hussein and his companions with that of those whoever killed in the protests against the Shah. Another visual stimuli to inflame the emotions of the demonstrators were

---

[42] Ruhollah Khomeini, "Statements about Muharram and Ashura, 1969," in *The Ashura Uprising in the Words and Messages of Imam Khomeini* (Tehran: The Institute for the Compilation and publication of Imam Khomeini's Works, 1995), 7.

[43] Jean-Charles Brotons, *US Officials and the Fall of the Shah* (Plymouth: Lexington Books, 2010), 64.

[44] Gary Sick, *All Fall Down*, 111.

[45] Amir Taheri, *The Spirit of Allah: Khomeini and the Islamic Revolution* (Bethesda: Adler & Adler, 1986), 321-322.

[46] Javier Gil Guerrero, *The Carter Administration & the Fall of Iran's Pahlavi Dynasty* (New York: Palgrave Macmillan, 2016), 145.

[47] Javier Gil Guerrero, *The Carter Administration & the Fall of Iran's Pahlavi Dynasty*, 151.

[48] Gholam Reza Afkhami, *The Life and Times of the Shah*, 486.

[49] Javier Gil Guerrero, *The Carter Administration & the Fall of Iran's Pahlavi Dynasty*, 145.

the white shrouds (*kaffan*) worn by some protesters.[50] By dressing themselves with the traditional shroud prepared for the dead, the demonstrators were making clear their readiness to die as martyrs.[51]

The demonstration gave Iranians the opportunity to be martyred on the same date that Hussein was killed. The protests against the Shah and the battle of Karbala were suddenly one and the same. To protest against the Shah was to fight in the way of Hussein.[52]

The marches of Tasua and Ashura were "awe-inspiring in their scale, orderliness and unity of purpose."[53] There were no torrents of blood. The demonstrations were well-organized, disciplined and mostly peaceful. "Hussein is our saviour, Khomeini is our leader," was one of the slogans of the rallies. Khomeini's call didn't go unheeded: hundreds of thousands attended the marches, which ended with the reading of a communiqué announcing the unity of the opposition under Khomeini's leadership. Thus, Ashura became the day in which Khomeini's command of the revolution was made official. In large part, that had been the result of Khomeini's masterful use of the Karbala paradigm, which had become a "crucible" that forged the "meanings of the symbols" that had endowed Khomeini with the aura of a divinely appointed guide.[54]

---

[50] Janet Afary and Kevin B. Anderson, *Foucault and the Iranian Revolution*, 103.

[51] CIA Directorate of Intelligence research paper, "Khomeinism: The Impact of Theology on Iranian Politics," Secret, November, 1983. NARA, CREST, CIARDP84S00927R000100150003-5.

[52] Ingvild Flaskerud, "Redemptive Memories: Portraiture in the Cult of Commemoration" in Pedram Khosronejad, *Unburied Memories: The Politics of Bodies of Sacred Defense Martyrs in Iran* (New York: Routledge, 2013), 25.

[53] Anthony Parsons, *The Pride & the Fall: Iran 1974-1979* (London: Jonathan Cape, 1984), 110.

[54] Rebecca Ansary Pettys, "The Ta'zieh: Ritual Enactment of Persian Renewal," *Theatre Journal*, Vol. 33, No. 3. (Oct., 1981), 341-354.

Conclusion

The novelty of Khomeini's approach to Muharram was not to make a political use of the religious rallies. Khomeini's transformative approach to Muharram was to dilute the boundaries between the religious ceremonies and the revolutionary process. It was an activist approach to Muharram: "Every month of the year is Muharram, every day of the year is Ashura and every piece of land is Karbala."[55]

Takia is the name of the structure specifically created for staging Tazieh performances before a large audience. Khomeini successfully liberated the Tazieh from its cage and turned Iran into a great takia in which every Muslim was no longer a spectator but an actor of an ongoing play. The Tazieh was no longer a representation of a past event but a foreshadowing of the Iranian revolution. During the Muharram of 1978 Iranians were both celebrating the Taziehs and taking part in an ongoing one. The whole country had been turned into a takia.

As Baqer Moin has stated, "the constant themes of sadness and morbidity in [Muharram's rituals] reflect the ever-present sense among the Shia that they are an oppressed community who had been wronged historically." What Khomeini added to that sense was the duty to seek revenge against those who had wronged the Imam.[56]

Khomeini offered Iranians the opportunity to move from a position of witness to that of participants. To forego the idea of passive weeping for Hussein and rescue the event from the past in order to transform the present.[57] The Iranians involved in the revolution were the true heirs of Hussein and those killed in the streets were martyrs like Hussein's companions. The proliferation of posters with the pictures of those killed made of them icons. They were no ordinary victims, they were martyrs. The process of sanctification of the deceased opposition mirrored the mourning of the victims of Karbala.[58]

Martyrdom was glorified and presented as the noblest form of struggle against oppression and social injustice. Exaltation of noble suffering and defiant embrace of death in the face of adversity and defeat. Hussein had given a meaning to the pain and adversity. Only through massive self-sacrifice could anyone expect big rewards in the afterlife and consider himself a true follower of the Imam.[59]

Khomeini's appropriation of the ceremonies of Muharram was an attempt

---

[55] Michael Axworthy, *Revolutionary Iran, A History of the Islamic Republic* (Oxford: Oxford University Press, 2013), 66.

[56] Baqer Moin, *Khomeini: Life of the Ayatollah* (London: I.B. Tauris, 199), 17.

[57] Michael M.j. Fischer and Mehdi Abedi (eds.), *Debating Muslims: Cultural Dialogues in Postmodernity and Tradition* (Madison: The University of Wisconsin Press, 1990), xxviii.

[58] Haggai Ram, "Multiple Iconographies: Political Posters in the Iranian Revolution," in Shiva Balaghi and Lynn Gumpert, *Picturing Iran: Art, Society and Revolution* (New York: I.B. Tauris, 2002), 95.

[59] Ervand Abrahamian, *Khomeinism: Essays on the Islamic Republic* (Berkeley: University of California Press, 1993), 29.

to banish the quietist approach to Shia Islam. Behind the struggle over Tazieh and Muharram was a battle for the soul of Shia Islam between its quietist and activist tendencies. The activist approach postulates the deep involvement of the clergy in politics in order to establish a true Islamic society. The quietists, on the other hand, advocate indirect or limited involvement in politics or no involvement at all. Unlike the activists, the quietist were prone to accommodate the secular authorities and to abandon themselves in the study of purely religious affairs. Although they defend the autonomy of the clergy from the government interference and even acknowledge the necessity of religious supervision of the state, they rejected any actual takeover of the institutions by the clergy. Their model was Imam Hassan, Hussein's elder brother, who had compromised with Muawiya in order to retire from politics. He had lived a quiet life away from the power struggles. Muharram and Tazieh are a vindication of Hussein and his activist approach, of the necessity to fight the usurpers, tyrants and infidels by force if necessary. As Khomeini said, "Islam is politics or it is nothing."[60]

---

[60] Bernard Lewis, *From Babel to the Dragomans: Interpreting the Middle East* (New York: Oxford University Press, 2004), 303.

Journal of South Asian and Middle Eastern Studies Vol. XL, No.2, WINTER 2017

The Role of the Discourse of Modernity/Backwardness in Motifs of Modern Persian Fictions

Saeed Honarmand*

Since Ākhundzādeh[1] most Persian fiction has been constructed around one motif, which we will call "revealing ignorance." This motif has a direct relationship to the discourse of Modernity/Backwardness, as do the solutions to the perceived problems of "ignorance" and "Backwardness" that have been offered. In fact, the motif arises from a specific interpretation of this discourse. Chronologically, the discourse appeared in the late mid-nineteenth century, when British and Russian political and military control over the country had reached its highest point. The discourse, in its main outline, was always an attempt to find the answers to two questions: In comparison to the Europeans, and the perception of the fact that we became backward, what is or was the main cause for that? second, how can we get out of this situation and become

---

* Saeed Honarmand is a lecturer and coordinator of the Persian department in The MESAAS Department at Columbia University. He has been teaching Persian language, literature, and Iranian mythology and culture as a Visiting Assistant Professor in the Department of Near Eastern Languages and Cultures at The Ohio State University. He has also been the director of the Persian Immersion Summer program at University of Wisconsin-Madison. He received his Ph.D. in comparative Studies from The Ohio State University.

[1] Mirzā Fath-ali Ākhundzādeh also known as Akhundov is considered as the first modern Persian story and play writer (1812-1878). He was considered the first "enlightened" (in the sense of deriving his opinions from the values of the European Enlightenment) figure in Persian literature. He was also a political writer who wrote several essays on modernity versus backwardness and ignorance. His parents prepared him for a career in Shi'a clergy, but the young man was attracted to the literature. Ākhundzādeh moved to Tbilisi, in today Georgia when he was 20 years old. There he worked as a translator of Oriental languages for the Russian government. His acquaintance and friendship with the Russian Decembrists played some part in formation of his so called Europeanized outlook. He published number of playwrights, a short novel as well as the three books on the Iranian politics and government. As an orientalist and a supporter of the Russian Empire he created an Iranian nationalistic narrative in which the pre-Islamic greatness of Iran was glorified before it was destroyed at "the hands of the hungry, naked and savage Arabs." It was through this discursive narrative that Akhundzada is considered as the forerunner of the modern Iranian nationalism. He is also counted as one of the founders of modern Iranian literature, and his influence is traceable through this discourse in such major Persian-language writers as Malkum Khan, Mirzā Agha Khan Kermāni and Mirzā Abd ul-Rahim Talibi. All of them were advocates of reforms in Iran around the Constitutional Revolution (1906-11).

a modern country? Although the answers to these questions have periodically been different, the formula that has shaped these debates has not changed at all.

This paper refers to this discourse in an attempt to categorize modern novels according to their functional motifs. The purpose of this paper, is threefold: first, to indicate the historical background and situation in which the discourse is formed; second, to outline the most characteristic elements of the discourse as well as the relationship between the discourse and the aforementioned motif: third, to categorize the major Persian novels under the different interpretations of the motif from Ākhundzādeh (d. 1878) to the young Beyzāi[2] in the 1980s. In this last analysis, the motif and the stories will be studied in relation to the political and cultural solutions that have been offered by political activists in general and secularists in particular.

Historical Background of Discourse

During the 19th century Iran in its confrontation with Western military[3] and then Western civilization, realized its own relative backwardness. As a solution to this problem of backwardness, the pursuit of military progress, industry, science, and later Western arts and culture became primary goals of Iranian society. To industrialize the country, according to these goals, two major solutions were considered: industrializing the military, and westernizing the culture. To refigure the modern history of Iran, a plot structure was borrowed from European historiography and this involved westernizing the culture. However, the geopolitical situation on the one hand, and the worn-out system of landowning made this almost impossible. At that time Iran was economically and militarily surrounded by three major powers: the Russians to the north, the British to the east and south, and the Ottomans to the west. Geopolitically, both Russia and Britain, as imperial powers neighboring countries and potentially of Iran itself, simply did not allow this industrialization to take place. Because of this situation reform was impossible in Iran.

After its military defeat by Russia in 1823, Iran realized its military and industrial weaknesses. In this situation, Prince Abbās Mirzā (1789-1833), the son of the second Qajar king Fathali Shah, was one of the first pioneers in the process of westernization. However, his only response to the problem was to strengthen Iran's military with newly developed weapons. To him and to other statesmen that was the only way to solve the problem. Also Iran started to have a close relationship with France, the enemy of the British and Russians alike. Nonetheless, Iran was not able to get either a military factory

---

[2] Bahrām Beizāi (1938-), playwright and director. He has won several international awards.
[3] The Wars between Russia and Iran, 1813 (Golastān treaty) and 1823 (Turkman Chāi treaty) and later with British in Bushehr and Herat (1848).

or modern weapons from France or any other country. Two decades later the prime minister, Amir Kabir (1807-1852), under Nāsser al-Din Shah tried to reform the financial system in order to establish new industries. Although unsuccessful in achieving his goal, Amir Kabir continued this process by founding the "Dār al-Fonnun" Institute,[4] which served the purpose of reforming the Iranian education system and training administrative leaders, as well as imposing controls on financial transactions.

But none of these efforts were successful, because, first, although it had not been occupied , Iran was still being controlled by the Russians and British, especially from the 1860's onward. And second, because the economy and social bonds and institutions were almost entirely ruined and there were not enough funds and experts to rebuild them.

Towards the end of the 19th century, the problem of backwardness entered the intellectual realm, and became a subject of intellectual debates. Disappointed by their corrupt government and king, intellectuals, religious and non-religious, tried to find solutions for the growing problem of backwardness. Religious movements such as Bābism (later Baha'ism), which saw the problem through the traditional discourse of messianic expectation, interpreted the situation as omens of the end of the millennium. This new religion of Bābism, which became the enemy of the central government, brought about talk of a kind of Islamic Protestantism in the context of religious reforms. Oppression and executions, however, were the results of this movement.

On the other hand, the dominant religious leaders who had close relationships with the royal family defined the problem through the old religious-political point of view. They, especially Seid Jamāl Asadābādi, known as Afghāni (1838-1897), contextualized it according to the Wars of the Crusades between Muslims and Christians. This categorization of Iran's perceived "backwardness" meant that Occidentalism became part and parcel of the ubiquitous presence and seductive lure of Islamist discourse. Asadābādi believed that hostile relations between the two great Islamic states, the Ottomans and Iranians, had led the European powers to take advantage of them. By visiting the capital cities of the two Islamic states, he tried to unite both countries under a greater nation of Islam in order to save the Islamic world from Western colonizers. In the mid 1890's he died in Istanbul and was buried there at a time that relations between European and Islamic countries were going from bad to worse.

Meanwhile, non-religious intellectuals, some of whom were statesmen, came up with different solutions by using a different discourse. Most of them came to the conclusion that Iran had no choice but to become westernized in order to overcome its backwardness. The grand narrative of progress,

---

[4] The House of Technologies, i.e. modern university.

modeled by the secularists on a perceived European narrative, created a genre of historiography in which the struggle between "tradition" and "modernity" became paramount. Statesmen such as Amin al-Duleh (1896-1898), the second prime minister of Mozafar al-Din shah, during his chancellorship, tried to formulate laws to address the problem according to the perspective and put these laws into effect; however, he was unsuccessful in this attempt, and had to leave office.

At the same time, secularists such as Mirzā Āgā Khān Kermāni (1854 —1896/97)[5], Abd al-Rahim Tālebov (1835-1911) and Mirzā Malkom Khān (1833-1908) proceeded to examine the issue from various social, cultural and political angles. From the political point of view, they demanded the establishment of a constitutional government alongside a European legal system, and thus they supported the Constitutional Movement. From the socio-cultural perspective, the problem of backwardness was perceived to be the result of illiteracy and irrationality, which were considered to be the cause of superstitious beliefs. Accordingly, literacy was the sign of modernity and orality, on the other hand, was seen as the cause of illiteracy and thus, equal to backwardness. By literacy, however, they meant the ability to read and understand European culture and literature. A consequence of this notion was that they saw, as some still see, traditional writers working in genres such as religious philosophy and so on, as ignorant. From this perspective, they in general drew a distinct line between the modern man, who was pro-Western and acted and thought like a European, and the ignorant one, who was a traditionalist and an anti-reformist.

Some of the intellectuals, following Ākhundzādeh, thought that superstitious beliefs stemmed solely from Islam. Ākhundzādeh was actually the first intellectual who discussed social reforms in terms of an Islamic Protestantism. He believed that the problem lay in Islamic superstitions, which according to him had been built up from the time of the reign of the Arabs in Iran, after the 7th century conquest, onward. It is important to note that most of these intellectuals, especially Ākhundzādeh, lived, at least for a few years of their lives, out of Iran, especially in Russia and Britain, or in the British-colonized countries of India and Egypt. The five so-called enlightened-men of Iran, Ākhundzādeh, Malkum Khān, Tālebov, Mirzā Āqā-khān, and Zen al-Abdin Marāqe'i (1840-1910), lived in Russia, Britain, Istanbul (Turkey), Alexandria (Egypt) and Tiblise/Istanbul, respectively. Their main journals were also published in Bombay, Alexandria, and Istanbul. Later on all of the intellectuals in this movement moved to Europe, especially to Berlin, Switzerland and London.

---

[5] *Andīsheh-hā-yi Mīrzā Āqā Khān Kermānī*. Saarbrücken, Germany: Inteshārāt-e Navīd, 1992.

46

Re-examining the concept of culture and religion was one way to discuss the issue. Enlightening the public about the progressive establishment of the West through the arts and media was another. Ākhundzādeh, in his book, *Letters* (Maktubāt), argues: "If we want to become a modern country, like European countries, we have to reform Islam, for this we have to have an Islamic Protestant movement to free women from the veil and let people learn about science and technology"[6]

However, a closer look at the meaning of the word "reform" reveals that, in this case, reform is seen primarily as a particular solution to the problem of backwardness. In other words reform is the means by which the end goal of the establishment of a civilized culture and a modern society is achieved. It is only in the context of this civilized culture in a modern society that people can gain freedom and prosperity. An important question that was directed to the intellectuals was the question of people's agency in determining their own interests. The response of Ākhundzādeh's, and others, was that the people were entrapped in their superstitious beliefs and uncivilized lifestyles and, thus, were unable to recognize and decide what was best for themselves.

As a result he, and the other intellectuals, came up with the idea of revealing to people their own ignorance, superstitious beliefs and uncivilized culture, on the one hand, and educating them about the civilized cultures and societies of the West on the other hand. And this became the main goal for literature, which had at this time become primarily political in its aims. Later it will be seen see that this was the formula that colonizers had also used in order to legitimize their policies towards the colonized countries.

Discourse of Modernity and Backwardness

But how did intellectuals come up with this idea or solution? Or how, in the first place, did this discourse emerge out of Iran's political situation? Modernity in Europe was an enlightenment project. But its notion as well as its function changed in Iran. For instance, the break from tradition became just a break from the dominant religion, Islam. There seem to be three different backgrounds to the Iranian formulation:

One goes back to the traditional role of Persian literature as a dispenser of advice in order to show the way to enlightenment and salvation, although there was never any sort of analytical discourse present in such works, at least not until the last decades of the 19th century. Intellectuals had traditionally always seen literature as in some sense a device to enlighten people or give them advice. Nonetheless, there was a national movement in the 1840's and onward called the literary movement, and some writers and poets, who were later on

---

[6] Ākhundzādeh, *Maktubāt: Political Letters*, 15-16.

47

called traditionalists, wanted to revive Iranian identity by going back to the first Persian literary traditions; among other things this meant using Persian or pre-Persian words, phrases, thoughts, and traditions in order to avoid and get rid of the Islamo-Arabic tradition. Some historical novels were written using this discourse, in which pre-Islamic Iran was glorified. By the end of the 19th century, however, another literary movement appeared. This movement, influenced by French revolutionary writers and thinkers, particularly by Montesquieu, Rousseau and Descartes, was a counter discourse to the former because it sought for the "real Iranian identity" through oral and colloquial tradition, in the way that Herder saw the oral tradition in Germany Bendix [7]. This movement was especially popular among the Iranian Turks as well as the Northern Azerbaijanis, who like pre-seventeenth century Germans among their European communities, did not have a written tradition in the Islamic world. This point leads to the second contextual background which involves the role of Iranian Turks in the constitutional revolution.

This second context goes back to progressive movements in Northern Azerbaijan, whose partition from Iran took place in the 1820's by way of the Russians, and to the modernization movement in the Ottoman Empire and later on that of the Young Turks on one hand, and, on the other to oral traditions versus the written traditions in Iran or Ottoman territories. The Ottoman Empire and Northern Azerbaijan were the first Islamic societies that directly encountered Western civilization. There can be seen the very same discourse of modernity/ backwardness as well as the identity discourse, and the most detailed arguments and discussions concerning the problem of backwardness/ignorance. Turks had ruled over most of the Islamic world for centuries, but during those centuries they used and promoted the Arabic and Persian religious and literary/written traditions instead of their own oral traditions. Now, in the light of the validation of oral traditions, which was itself drawn from European models, they embedded the whole discourse of modernity/ backwardness in a popular character name Mollā Nasr al-Din; this happened especially in Northern Azerbaijan which had a close relationship with the Russian revolutionaries. The Mollā Nasr al-Din character is a shared production of the Islamic world, but as far as the evidence shows, Iranians didn't use him in a political context – at least, not before the Constitutional Revolution – as a means of revealing the political ignorance of the people. He is a dual character, a fool and smart at the same time, who characterizes people's stupidity and their smartness simultaneously. He was so popular in the late 19th and early 20th centuries that one of the major revolutionary newspapers in

---

[7] Bendix, Regina. *In Search of Authenticity*. Madison, Wis.: University of Wisconsin Press, 1997 (chapter 1).

the Constitutional Revolution was named after him. Since Ākhundzādeh and Tālebov were originally Turks and the influence of Mollā Nassr al-Din on them, in that context, was natural, characters could be seen as modeled on him in both Ākhundzādeh's and Tālebov's works, such as *Tamsilāt* and *ketāb*-e *Ahmed*.

By the early 20th century the distinction between these movements grew deeper. For the revival movement the only way to a modern future was by going back to pre-Islamic times; whereas the colloquial movement, if you will, saw the past, as embodied in either the Islamic or Iranian traditions, as an obstacle to the progressive movement, namely to adopting the Europeans culture. The sharp distinction between the heritage and colloquial traditions among the traditionalists and modern intellectuals, since the mid-19th century, is similar to the way Kirshenblatt-Gimblett describes the phenomenon in her essay, "Theorizing Heritage."[8] The gap between them grew deeper in the 20th century, and further gaps appeared within the two movements themselves. There are now four sharply divided groups in today's Iran: with leftists and pro-Westerners on one side, and nationalists and Islamists on the other side. In terms of literary narrative the leftists, pro-Westerners and nationalists are close, although the old distinction is still there beneath everything, even in the poetic devices used in every line of their literary productions. In terms of political narrative, nationalists fall between Islamists and pro-Westerners (secularists) in general. Here again the archaic language versus the colloquial indicates where the line is drawn, and this approaches to the theory of the Great Divide, literacy versus orality, but of course in completely reverse fashion. A process like one Franz Fanon has conceptualized provides a useful analogy, when he describes "folklore as a stage to pass through in the creation of a post-colonial national culture." He delineates this sequence as follows: "first, native intellectuals embrace the colonial legacy; then, they valorize native traditions; finally, they reject both in an effort to create a new national culture."[9] There is no doubt that modern Iranian novelists, who are dominantly leftists, or as they claim now modernists, depict Iranian culture in general through Western lenses, as can be seen by the fact that the motif of "revealing ignorance" remains a dominant feature in their novels. Nevertheless, as Fanon says, the process is now in its third stage, that of creating a new national culture, which in the last 50 years has merged with the strong literary tradition. It is especially obvious among the recent writers, such as Beizā'i, who believe the roots of backwardness to be in the traditional culture, rather than anywhere else.

This third background can be considered according to the discourse of

---

[8] Kirshenblatt-Gimblett, "Theorizing Heritage," Ethnomusicology: Journal of the Society for Ethnomusicology, 1995. Vol. 39, No. 3, fall: p. 369-390.

[9] Fanon, Frantz. "On National Culture." *In the Wretched of the Earth.* 1968. Translated by Constance Farigan, 206-48. New York: Grove. 1968.

Orientalism, and the idea of modernity/backwardness could well have been originally created by colonialism in the first place. Iranians, overall, have seen it as the attitude of the West towards the Eastern cultures and societies. This attitude is in fact magnified in the early works such as Montesquieu's *Lettres persanes* (*Persian Letters*, 1721), and *The Adventures of Hajji Baba of Ispahan* (1824) or *The History of Persia* written by James Morier and John Malcolm respectively in which the Iranians in general were introduced as non-educated, superstitious, and non-ethical people. It is worth mention that Montesquieu's work was primarily a criticism of contemporary France through imagined Persian eyes; but Iranians interpreted reversely. The Iranian intellectuals adopted this idea through these works as well as Ākhundzādeh's plays and stories. Morier's novel was translated in the late nineteenth century by Mirzā Habib Isfahāni into very fluent colloquial Persian and its style and structure became a norm among later writers/political activists. The story depicts an array of superstitious, uncivilized, lazy characters who don't have real jobs and don't want to have any either. The main character is an ignorant man, but, according to his own claim, people think of him as a doctor and magician. The function of the book is to stereotype Iranians as backward people who need the European's help in order to overcome this backwardness and become citizens of a modern country – the same much utilized colonial narrative that can be found in India and Egypt. As a comparison, the novel contains a few prototypical Western characters who are rational and educated. The story is told to a westerner in Istanbul by an educated Iranian official in order to describe his own people's ignorance. It is interesting that the translator was one of the activists during the constitutional movement. And it's not a coincidence that at that time writers such as Isfahāni, who is thought to be the probable translator of the book, were the ones who raised the problem of backwardness.

Around this time there are some stories in Persian, plays and poetry, which also deal with the problem of backwardness. An examination of these works shows one central motif, which has shaped plots and characters. This central motif is the aforementioned "revealing ignorance" which corresponds to the main problem articulated by the discourse and is also to be found in Morier's novel. Works such as *Allegories* (Tamsilāt) by Ākhundzādeh written in the last decades of his life (d. 1970), most of Jamālzādeh's works written in early 1920s, and some of Hedāyat's, such as *The Lady Alavieh* (Alavieh Khānom) written in 1930s, as well as the Deh-khodā's *The Nonsensical* (Charand O Parand) published in the *Sur-e Esrāfil* during the Constitutional Revolution (1906-1909), are formed specifically around this motif.

In these works there is the very same pattern or story setting found in Morier's work, namely a modern man, a European or an Iranian with a European education, versus an ignorant, traditional one. At the end, the theme falls into the pattern of *self* and *other*. But the difference here is crucial, because *self* is in fact an Iranian man with the European "mask" on his face and the *other* is also an Iranian man, but a traditional one, who is looked down upon for not having European education and manner. From this perspective modernism is not a complex socio-historical era but rather a simple concept that could happen if people, one by one or all together, simply start to be and think like Westerners. Here a question to ask is: Is this discourse, as Fanon or Edward Said believed, created by European orientalists or formed within and by the particular situation of Iran? The discourse, in fact, has some very native characteristics; however, it also shares its main motifs and concepts with those of all colonized countries in Asia and Africa.

But the discourse of the European man versus the backward Iranian one has had a special, somewhat different, impact on Iran as well as on the other Islamic countries, because the impact of the discourse can be traced to the historic conflict between the Christian and Islamic worlds. As well as the backward/modern motif, as Ale Ahmad points out in his *Dar khedmat o kheyānat-e roshanfekrān*[10] and Joubin echoes in her article, "Islam and Arabs through the Eyes of the Encyclopedia: The "Other" as a Case of French Cultural Self-Criticism," there was the anti-Islamic rhetoric that was used by the revolutionary French writers. In the first case, Muslims were demonized; whereas in the second case their religion was depicted as superstitious and backward. Joubin believes that French writers used Islam instead of Christianity deliberately in order to avoid the direct conflict with the church institutions in France.[11]

As could be seen the causes and solutions are not consistent with each other at all. The discourse under these interpretations does not have a three dimensional perspective considering all aspects of the historical situation. First neither of them can be the major cause for anything. It is rather a way of problematization in which the historical circumstances are reduced into simple solutions under the concepts of progress and backwardness. Suggested solutions, such as getting rid of Islamic superstitions, replacing the Arabic alphabets with the Roman ones, or reviving the pre-Islamic beliefs namely Zoroastrianism instead of Islam, are seen as the way out of backwardness. Second, the solutions can hardly touch reality in terms of possibility. For instance, the cause for the situation of backwardness goes back to the Arab invasion of Iran. So in order to solve the problem, some of the writers have come up with the solution that Iranians have to change their religion and go back to pre-Islamic culture and religion. This

---

[10] Ale Ahmad, *Dar khedmat o kheyānat-e roshanfekrān*, 35.

[11] Joubin, Rebecca. "*Islam and Arabs through the Eyes of the Encyclopedia: The 'Other' as a Case of French Cultural Self-Criticism*", International Journal of Middle East Studies, 2000, Vol. 23, No. 2. Pp. 240-261.

solution is obviously an impossible requirement. And even if this were possible our information on pre-Islamic Iran is limited and for the most part scattered with respect to language as well as discourse, so it is unclear what the culture would be returning to. Even though the culture has altered completely since the pre-Islamic period, and it would be impossible to revive the past, there are still intellectuals, especially among the nationalists-secularists, who promote this kind of discourse.

According to the ways of problematization, there are three solutions in order to get out of backwardness and become a modern society: First, reform in Islam, which was raised in the first phase of the movement, Akhundzādeh and later Jamālzādeh suggest this solution in their works. Second, replacing Islam by Zoroastrianism in the second phase and especially after the Constitutional Revolution; influenced by Mirzā Āghā Khān, Hedāyat's works are shaped by this concept. And finally, dropping the whole culture altogether, including the religion, and adopting a completely Western culture, science, and even mythology and so on. A number of writers represented this solution in their works either in a moderate or extreme ways. There is, however, one exception; no one has yet suggested replacing Islam with Christianity. The reason for that could be the enlightenment in Europe, which influenced 19th century Iranian intellectuals and was itself skeptical of Christianity as a civilizing force.

Different Motifs, Different Novels

In order to narrativize the discourse in these works writers usually form their stories based on two opposite types of characters. One, as was mentioned earlier, is educated, rational, and westernized; and the other is exactly the opposite: uneducated, traditional, and superstitious. Some of these stories were just about one character, either educated or ignorant. The author's purpose was simply to show or reveal the idiotic things that the superstitious character does to himself, to others and to his country. The main goal of authors, in these stories, is to show the necessity of reforming religion and culture.

After the constitutional movement of 1906-1911, different responses to the discourse brought about four more motifs alongside the central one. Ignorance was and still is the main cause for backwardness in these four motifs, but the causes and therefore the solutions are defined differently. For example, in the second motif the nationalistic elements of the discourse, from the early revival movement, bring another argument into the picture. Here it is seen that the cause of ignorance is not superstitious beliefs but Islam itself. In the third and fourth motifs, both derived from the central one, religion as the cause of backwardness. In this case religion does not just refer to Islam, but also includes other religions. These motifs can be seen as encapsulated in Marx's famous notion of religions as the opium of the people.

The second motif was shaped after the First World War. At this time, the Iranian identity crisis takes a large place in the discourse. As a result, the motif now shifts from reforming culture and religion to replacing them with their ancient Persian equivalents. Under this discourse, some intellectuals and writers such as Hedāyat started to blame Islam for the problem of backwardness. They deemed getting rid of Islam was not just the best solution but also the only solution to the problem. Their solutions, however, were divided into two groups: replacing Islam by the ancient religion of Zoroastrianism, and replacing it by western culture and literature.

Hedāyat [12]shows the backwardness of Islam and Arabic culture in books such as *Mr. Hājji* (Hājji Āgā), *On Islamic Rising* (Fi-Be'sat al-Islamieh), and *The Pearl Cannon* (Toup-e Morvāri). Meanwhile he glorifies pre-Islamic civilization, culture and even religion in works like *Parvin the Daughter of Sāsān* (Parvin Doukhtar-*e* Sāsān), *Non-Iranians* (Anirān) and so forth. Also in the *Blind Owl*, his most famous work[13], Hedāyat deals with the same motif, with the only difference being that he problematizes the issue and tries to see other causes as also being operative. In this period love stories such as *Frightening Tehran* (Tehran-e Makhuf) by Moshfeq Kāzemi and romantic poetry were published, but mainstream literature did not take them seriously.

After the Second World War the central motif takes on another dimension. Marxism, which was the paradigm of the ideology at that time, considered the ignorance problem in terms of class theory. *Self* and *other* for most Marxists and other leftists of those decades were confused terms. For the pro-Moscow Marxists *other* was the Iranian government as well as the US, whereas for the moderate Socialists such as Ale Ahmad, who was also a story-writer using this formula, *other* was, under the influence of Fanon, the West and East. There were also right-wing modernists tied with the pro-American government of the time that saw the "people" of Iran as the *other*; but their literary productions did not follow the discourse in the main principals. For this reason, their works did not affect main stream readers in Iran at all.

According to the leftists in general the working class was not aware of its own interests because the upper class, especially those in power, did not allow this. As was mentioned, at this stage the main enemy was not considered to be religion or culture. The focus was instead shifted to colonialism and imperialism along with the domestic upper class. Therefore the struggle was perceived to be between the upper class and its foreign supporters on one hand

---

[12] Hedāyat, Ṣādeq and Mas'ud Farzād. *Vaq vaq sāhāb*. Tehrān: Amīr Kabīr, 1341 [1962].
[13] Hedāyat, Ṣādeq. *Buf-e Kur* (The Blind Owel). Tehrān: Enteśārāt-e Amir Kabeer, 1335 [1956].

and the working class on the other hand. Bozorg Alavi[14] was the first writer who used this perception in stories such as "Gilāni Man" (Gileh Mard) and *Her Eyes* (Cheshmhāyash), although earlier there were some stories such as *The Frightening Tehran* (Tehrān-e Makhouf) that vaguely showed a sense of class. Social realism had a big influence on the backwardness motif, and writers like Ahmed Mahmood, Doulatābādi, Sā'edi, even Ale Ahmed and Dāneshvar, among others have utilized this form of the motif.

From the 1960's onward, a fourth motif was derived from the third one. This motif was based on the same theory, but it has one big difference from the third one. In the third motif, mostly seen are three sorts of characters: an activist or intellectual, a character from the working class, and an upper class character. The main theme is to reveal the poverty of the working class, and the money and the power that the upper class character has stolen from them. At the same time the character from the intellectual or working class is an activist, who shares the political views of the writer. The activist tries to reveal who the real exploiters of the working class are, and how one must engage in a struggle against them. Because of censorship the themes became more dramatic, more complicated, and more metaphorical. And as a result the fourth motif was derived from the third one. The forth motif deals with only two types of characters: an activist or an intellectual and a *Sāvāki*, or a member of Shah's police or agent. And the theme is the fight or struggle between these two, in some stories, and the revelation of the criminal acts of the regime against intellectuals in others. As a contrast to the third motif there is hardly a working class character in this fourth version. In terms of genre, the fourth one tended to be narrated in a tragic manner; whereas the third one was more epical and optimistic in tone. Here the author has changed his position vis-à-vis the reader of the story. The story is written so that the author can show or teach him about the regime. Some plays and novels of Sā'edi, Golshiri, Ale Ahmed, and Barāheni are constructed around this motif.

After the 1979 revolution new issues, such as the legal system and women's rights brought out other aspects of the motif as well as a modification of the discourse. Although the motif was still the same, it had incorporated into itself new issues such as women's rights and the defects of the judiciary discourse and legal system. For example, the women's rights movement has been significant in the development of some post 1979 works. In these works writers are concerned with the condition of women under Islamic law, and the rights they should have. But again we see works that were formed by the motifs mentioned above. Novels, like *Tobā and the Meaning of the Night*, and *Women*

---

[14] 'Alavī, Bozorg. *Chashmhāyash*. Tehrān: Mu'assasah-i Intishārāt-e Amīr Kabīr, 1357 [1978 or 1979].

Without Men by Shahrnush Pārsipur, or *Steel Heart* (Del-e Follād) by Moniru Ravānipur, as well as movies like *Two Women* written and directed by Tahmineh Milāni, are formed with the fourth, second and first motifs, but with a small difference; for example, in *Two Women*, men are ignorant and women want to educate themselves. Here the motif is combined with the wide-spread motif of "you write or you are killed." This motif is derived from A *Thousand and One Nights*, as articulated by Todorov[15] and based on its central female character of it, Shahrzād (Scheherazade), a work which became popular in the 1980's and 1990's.[16] Examining these works, see the central motif is transformed into these new arenas. Here, it is the traditional and patriarchal culture that was regarded as the cause of ignorance and backwardness. Opposing this traditional culture, iconoclasts adopted an "intellectual culture", which was a combination of some elements of Western and Persian cultures. For example the struggle between traditionalists and iconoclasts is apparent in works such as *The Symphony of Death* (Samphoni-e Mordegān) or *The Year of the Rebel* (Sal-e Balvā) by Javād Ma'rufi or *Tobā and the meaning of the night*. Even though they take place in the early medieval period, screenplays such as Bahrm Beizā'i's *Toumār-e Shakh Sharzin* and *Pardi-e Ne'i*, are based on this conflict.

In conclusion, all one can say is that although "revealing ignorance" as a theme does still exist, some writers are seeking other possibilities in new discourses, such as in new definitions of law and women's rights. However, the central motif of "revealing ignorance" or other derived motifs are still used to address new issues in a simple way. In fact, we reach the borderline of two eras, with two different types of attitudes towards the discourse and the motifs becoming apparent. While writers such as Arāmesh Doostdār or Shojā' al-Din Shafā are returning back to the early formula in their essays and see the religion of Islam as the main cause for backwardness, there are also some writers such as Shāygān[17] that try to study the phenomenon in a larger picture. And as stated before, alongside writers who used the motifs mentioned above, are seen some works that are different. Beizā'i's *Death of the King*, which deals with two opposite interpretations of the law, by the upper class on one hand and the working class on the other hand, is one of these works that does not use any of those motifs mentioned before. There is no definition for ignorance or backwardness as a theme or character in Beizā'i's work. His characters are smart and know what they are doing. They plan and set things together to get out of crises. Even

---

[15] Todorov, Tzvetan. 1977. *The Poetics of Prose*. Translated by Richard Howard, Ithaca, N.Y. : Cornell University Press, 1977.

[16] Slyomovics, Susan. *The Performance of Human Rights in Morocco*. Philadelphia: University of Pennsylvania Press, c2005. P.148

[17] Shayegan, Daryush. *Cultural schizophrenia: Islamic societies confronting the West*; translated from the French by John Howe, London: Saqi Books, 1992.

though at the end of the play, the Arabs come and ruin everything, and there seems to be a return to the second motif, the Arab invasion is not a crucial theme and can be easily removed from the play.

There is also a short story by Golshiri, named "The Caravan of Camels" that deals with Islamic law and its consequences in society. In this story, he shifts the discourse into a new direction. Not only does he enter the discourse of human law (secularist discourse) versus God's law (Islamist discourse), but he also makes the human law problematic. *Āyeneh-hāi Dardār* is another one of Golshiri's works which is formed differently. In this work, the main motif is the opposite interpretation of the origin of the story of Adam and Eve, and how Eve was created from Adam's rib. Golshiri, in this novella, puts the woman back in her real position, as the one who gives birth to the man, and not vice versa. Another motif, which is used in this work, is the motif of "story or death" mentioned above. To politicize the motif Golshiri added a new dimension to it. He equated death with silence, and storytelling with narrating the situation of intellectuals and activists to the coming generations.

Journal of South Asian and Middle Eastern Studies Vol. XL, No.2, WINTER 2017

Confronting the Symbol of the Intellectual: Sa'adallah Wannus's *Historical Miniatures* and the Legacy of Ibn Khaldun

Nezar Andary*

Historical figures like Ibn Khaldun have become symbols of past Arab's intellectual grandeur on the global stage. The conferences, book editions, street names, and dedications with Ibn Khaldun's name demonstrates that he is not only an intellectual to be studied, but also a figure to be manipulated. When *Historical Miniatures (Munamnamaat Tarikhiyah)* was first published in 1996, intellectuals from many parts of the Arab world were moved that a historical figure like Ibn Khaldun might be presented on stage, but more importantly that he could be criticized. The critics immediately tied Sa'adallah Wannus' play to a chronic Arab condition.

This paper argued that with *Historical Miniatures,* Wannus reevaluated a well-known historical event and symbol of Ibn Khaldun to define the role of intellectual in society. This revaluation provoked a cultural intervention that imagined a new way of confronting history and historiography itself.

Background of Sa'adallah Wannus: Radical Playwright to Late Stylist

Sa'adallah Wannus, who died in 2000, is a preeminent Arab playwright who wrote during the last part of the 20th century. Although his plays are still widely

* Nezar Anzary earned his PhD from UCLA Nezar Andary is an Assistant Professor of Film and Literature at Zayed University in the College of Humanities and Sustainability Sciences. From 2012-2014 he served as co-chair of the Middle East Caucus for the Society of Cinema and Media Studies organization. He has published literary translations, poetry, articles on Arab documentary, and most recently worked on a narrative of teaching the book Orientalism in four different languages. Nezar directed a multilingual play for the Abu Dhabi Book Fair and organized an Environmental Documentary Series. He also directed a documentary theatre project, "Memories of Childhood," worked as cultural mentor and producer for the Arab Film Studio. His article on well-known journalist Anthony Shadid will be published in Alif Journal in Spring 2017.

produced and ignite debate across the Arab states,[1] the works of this intellectual have received little scholarly notice in English. Chosen as official spokesman for UNESCO International Theatre Day in 1996, Wannus addressed the importance of theatre, criticized the intellectual climate in the Arabic-speaking world and confronted the sense of failure commonly shared many intellectuals committed to theatre around the world. He tied the loss of theater to "part of a crisis that encompasses culture in general." he saved a culture under siege as people embraced "a growing night life, colored screens, and packaged trivialities."[2]

Prolific after the 1967 war, Wannus took a hiatus from writing plays 1979-1988. In one interview, he cited choosing 1988 as the year he returned to writing drama together with the fall of the Soviet Union and Francis Fukuyama's statement on the end of History. He commented that he wanted to understand history better.[3] Between 1988 and 1998, he wrote six plays confronting the crucial inability of Arab culture "to come to terms with its own failures, contradictions, and history."[4]

His early plays *Haflat Samar min ajl khamsa Hizayran* (Evening Part for the fifth of June) and *Alfil ya Malak azzaman* (It's the Elephant, Dear King) introduced radical structures into Arabic theatre. Wannus adopted "Experimental theater," a form that had matured in Europe as exemplified by the works of Bertolt Brecht. However, experimentation was not adopted by Wannus in its original European forms. Unlike Samuel Beckett, Wannus chose not to be elitist and formal; but instead researched experimentation to find a theater style that fulfilled the needs of society as he saw them. He writes: "Isn't it possible for Arabic theatre to resurrect forms indigenous to our own storytelling with the influences we have learned from modern European theatre?"[5] He sought to create an experimental yet realistic theater that effectively spoke to specific sociopolitical conditions. Wannus' use of classical Arabic language has been called "revolutionary" for the way he created a formal language that was closer to colloquial Arabic. Some of his most powerful plays were written as interactive theater, such as *The Elephant, The King of All Times* (1969), *The Adventure of Jaber's Head*

---

[1] The first detailed readings of one of his later plays published in English is in Joseph Massad, *Desiring Arabs* (Chicago: University of Chicago, 2007). Wannus' plays have been translated into English by Salma Khadra al-Jayyusi's Translation project (Prota) **LIST THEM and into many languages across Europe and Japan. An earlier study of his work is by Roger Allen, "Arabic Drama in Theory and Practice: The Writings of Sa 'adallah Wannus," *Journal of Arabic Literature* 15 (1984): 94–113.

[2] Saadallah Wannus, *al-'Amal al-Kamila*, [complete works] vol. 3(Damascas: Dar al-Mada: 2002), 467.

[3] Interview with Sa'adallah Wannus conducted by Mari Elias, *at-Tariq* 1, 31 (January–February 1996): 96.

[4] Interview with Maison Ali, *As-Safir*, September 9, 1997, 24.

[5] Sa'adallah Wannus, *Al-Masrah wa Afaqihi*[Theatre and its Horizons] (Damascus: Dar Al Farabi, 1997), 33.

(1970), *The King is the King* (1977), and *Hanthala's Journey from Slumber to Consciousness* (1978). In these plays, Wannus introduced improvisation, live music and song, storytelling, and even direct conversation in order to have live interaction with the audience. The playwright managed to grant his audience the chance to make moral judgments and openly take sides on issues even before leaving the theater hall. He writes: "Our audiences need to see theatre not as some imposed Western structure, but rather an organic form able to adapt to our own cultural heritage."[6]

Wannus belonged to a movement called "Arab Theatre and Tradition"[7] which specifically advocated recreating historical models of Arab drama to speak to the present. Early in his career, Wannus identified himself as a Marxist. His penchant for critiques of elite economies never ended, although by the end of his career he became a more independent thinker. Two very recent English language studies have discussed Wannus at some length. He is vilified as an apologist for Arab nationalism by Fouad 'Ajami in *Dream Palaces of Arab Intellectuals*[8] and criticized as a proponent of Western liberalism by Massad in *Desiring Arabs*.[9] These portrayals of Wannus exemplify how Arab intellectual figures or symbols can be appropriated on two ends of an ideological spectrum that perhaps say more about current interpretative methods in Western study of the Arab world than about Wannus's contributions to intellectual debates in the Arab world. Wannus's representation on Ibn Khaldun must be examined to understand how cultural symbols in the Arab/Islamic world are negotiated and appropriated. For the purpose of this essay, it is necessary to discuss the meaning of Ibn Khaldun and understand the historical background to the play.

Ibn Khaldun: A Dynamic Historic Symbol

Ibn Khaldun's theories of state and society and his writings on kingship have been studied by scholars from diverse countries and disciplines.[10] His personality and work have been at the center of many debates.[11]. In his comprehensive *A History of the Arab Peoples*, Albert Hourani begins with a prologue on the life of Ibn Khaldun; for Hourani, ibn Khaldun's life represents a model for the

---

[6] Wannus, *Al-Masrah*, 41.

[7] See Yusif Qahwahji, "al-Masrah al-'Arabi wa Turath," *Dar al-Adab* 31, no. 6 (November 2001), 20–28.

[8] Fouad Ajami, *Dream Palaces of Arab Intellectuals* (New York: Random House, 2002).

[9] Joseph Massad, *Desiring Arabs* (Chicago: University of Chicago Press, 2007).

[10] The best-known by Ibn Khaldun is his *The Muqaddimah An Introduction to History,* trans. Franz Rosenthal, Bollingen Series XLIII (Princeton: Princeton University Press, 1967); and Ibn Khaldun, Abu Zaid 'Abdel Rahman Ibn Muhammad, *Al-Muqaddimah* [Prolegomena] (Tunis: Al-dar at-Tunisiyya, 1984).

[11] See Aziz al-Azmeh, *Ibn Khaldun in Modern Scholarship* (London: I.B Tauris, 1981); and Tarif Khalidi, *Arabic Historical Thought in the Classical Period* (Cambridge: Cambridge University Press, 1994).

whole field of Arab history.[12] Ibn Khaldun traveled all over what is now called the Middle East, met with many political leaders, wrote on numerous subjects, and suffered many hardships. Hourani begins his study with Khaldun because more than any other Arab and Islamic philosopher he traverses the disciplines of academic western universities; many Ibn Khaldun centers for learning and politics stretch across the world from the United States to Egypt, Turkey and Pakistan.

Aziz al-Azmeh calls the "universalist" conception of Ibn Khaldun as a thinker unfortunate because it detaches Khaldun from his specific theories.[13] Azmeh's classic book on Khaldun deserves mention because he narrates over a century of Orientalist work that manipulated Khaldun in diverse ways.[14] Wannus, too, knew how much Ibn Khaldun's work connected to many worldly discourses, and that to make him a character in a play would give him entry into many intellectual debates across the globe. *Historical Miniatures* represented the first examination of Ibn Khaldun's personal role as an intellectual, placing an almost sacred figure under a microscope. Instead of focusing on Ibn Khaldun's accomplishments as most historians do, Wannus chose to focus on his survivalist instincts and how he ingratiated himself to whatever leader happened to be in power.

During Ibn Khaldun's life, the plague severely affected large areas of the world; both of his parents died from the plague, and it influenced his worldview for the rest of his life.[15] The age of Ibn Khaldun witnessed major political changes in North Africa and al-Andalus. He wandered from palace to palace and city to city, and his adventures and experiences included the complicated politics of al-Andalus, Morocco, Cairo, and Damascus. He became a man without loyalty to one government, people, or even any one system of Islam. At an early age he was respected for his skills as a writer and for his ability to communicate with the Bedouins and other rural peoples.

Ibn Khaldun developed strong connections with the sultans of his age. Historians note that he played an important role for the ruler of Granada in negotiating with enemy leaders like Peter (al-Mukhif) of Castille.[16] In Granada, Ibn Khaldun was given land and met with many well-known scholars of al-Andalus including the well-known writer Ibn al-Khatib. Due to the turbulence of the times in al-Andalus, Ibn Khaldun moved to Fez and then to Cairo. He

---

[12] Albert Hourani, *A History of Arab Peoples* (Boston: Belknap, 1992), 1–4.

[13] Aziz Al-Azmeh, *Ibn Khaldun: An Essay in Reinterpretation* (Budapest: Central University Press, 2003), 154.

[14] Azmeh reviews how Ibn Khaldun was especially debated around the two poles of reason and belief. He cites M. Mahdi's *Ibn Khaldun's Philosophy of History* (London and Chicago: N.P., 1957) that promoted Ibn Khaldun as a pure philosopher as opposed to a religious thinker. Azmeh reveals how Ibn Khaldun has also been studied in relationship to mystical Sufi thought.

[15] Ibid., 23.

[16] Lacoste, *Al-'Allamah*, 58.

remained in Cairo for most of his life and produced many of his great works there. In Cairo, Ibn Khaldun found himself welcomed again by scholars and finally became close to Sultan Barquq, who later rewarded him with a position as a judge. Inan points out that Ibn Khaldun focused on his teaching and writing despite the vicissitudes of his political life.[17]

Wannus portrayed the next sultan Ibn Khaldun worked for, Al-Nasr Faraj, in *Historical Miniatures*, which begins a few weeks before the arrival of the sultan to Damascus with his entourage including Ibn Khaldun. During Al-Faraj's reign, Timurlane and the Tatars seized and plundered Aleppo, plunging Egypt and areas of the Fertile Crescent into waves of fear and hysteria. Al-Faraj, who was the son of the former sultan, insisted that Ibn Khaldun come with him to Damascus to deal with the impending threat.

While the outer city had surrendered to Timurlane, the main fortress (what is known today as the Old City) had not given in to the Tatar forces. According to his own writings, the only historical source, Ibn Khaldun decided to confront Timurlane on his own initiative.[18] During the meeting, the two discussed through a translator how Damascus would completely surrender and how much Ibn Khaldun knew of the Maghrib. According to Ibn Khaldun, Timurlane said:

> This does not convince me. I [Timurlane] want you to write on everything about the lands of the Maghrib — from its rivers, mountains, villages and cities — as I see it firsthand. And I [Ibn Khaldun] said: 'This will be done in your honor and I wrote it for him after I left his majlis.'[19]

After this meeting, Ibn Khaldun helped convince the leaders of Damascus to surrender the entire city to Timurlane.[20] In another meeting, Ibn Khaldun further recalled telling Timurlane:

> May God support you. I have been waiting 34 years to meet you. The translator Abd Jabar asked me, "What is the reason?" I responded: 'First, you are the Sultan of the World and the King of the universe and I do not think there has been a *khalifah* like you since the time of Adam. Second, I heard much about you from scholars and astrologers from the Maghrib.'[21]

Ibn Khaldun also referred to his meetings with other Damascenes and Timurlane on how to capture the main fortress of the city; Timurlane asked about

---

[17] Inan writes that Ibn Khaldun's fortunes were connected to the Sultan Barquq, who also was always being challenged and threatened.

[18] Ibn Khaldun, *At-Taarif bi Ibn Khaldun*, 411

[19] Ibn Khaldun, *At-Taarif bi Ibn Khaldun*, 411.

[20] 'Inan, *Ibn Khaldun*, 91.

[21] Ibn Khaldun, *At-Taarif bi Ibn Khaldun*, 414.

the different waterways and the weaknesses in the architectural structures of the last-held fortress in Damascus. Some historical sources indicate that Ibn Khaldun asked to be part of Timurlane's entourage, and while Timurlane did not accept, his offer, he did not stop his contacts with Ibn Khaldun.[22] According to his writings, Ibn Khaldun also presented Timurlane with presents such as sweets and carpets, and received money from Timurlane on his way back to Egypt.[23] There, Ibn Khaldun lived and continued producing seminal texts of Arab and Islamic history.

Ibn Khaldun in Wannus' *Historical Miniatures*:
The Role of the Intellectual

Sa'adallah Wannus' *Munamnamaat Tarikhiyah* (*Historical Miniatures*)[24] begins with an intellectual who is a known follower of Ibn Rushd, on a cross lamenting his books being burned[25] after a series of events that lead to the collapse of Arab powers in Damascus. *Historical Miniatures* is based on the fall of Damascus to the invading Mongol armies of Timurlane in the fifteenth Century.[26] The play begins Timurlane's army approaching and seizing the gates of Damascus and ends with the final capitulation of the Arab and Muslim forces to the Central Asian leader. Many other Arab literary and cinematic works evoke scenes of book burning.[27] Placing book burning as a central event within a narrative construction emphasizing a threat to intellectual rights and knowledge.

Although set in the fifteenth-century Damascus, the debates and images in *Historical Miniatures* had a pressing historical urgency for Arab intellectual in the later 1990s.[28] One intellectual is a martyr like the Gypsy singer Marwan, and the European scholar in Yusuf Chahin's film *Destiny*, Jamal ad-Din ash-Shariji screams his final words as he hangs from the cross:

---

[22] 'Inan, *Ibn Khaldun*, 93.

[23] Ibid., 94.

[24] Sa'adallah Wannus, *Munamnamaat Tarikhiyah* (Beirut: Dar al Adab, 1996).

[25] A prominent feature of Nidal Ashqar's staged performance of the play in November 1996 in Beirut was the burning of books.

[26] In English and European literature, many have been fascinated by Timurlane such as the well known example, Christopher Marlowe's play *Tamburlaine the Great* (Oxford: Oxford University Press, 1992). The invasion of Damascus is much a part of Arab/Islamic folklore. The events are as follows: Invading Syria, Timurlane took Aleppo and sacked it, and descended on Damascus, the second city of the Mamluk Empire, whose garrison had already been destroyed in a rash sortie. The governor held out with some forty men in the citadel, but surrendered after a month. Timurlane extorted a huge ransom from the town and then let his men loose to rape and pillage. Many of the inhabitants were viciously tortured, bastinadoed, burned or crushed in presses, and many were enslaved. See Abd al-Aziz Duri, *al-Juzur at-tarikhiyya lil-qawmiyya al-'arabiyya*, [Historical Roots of Arab Nationalism] (Beirut: Dar at-tali'a, 1984), 44–49.

[27] Several notable examples include: Radwa 'Ashur's *Thulathiyat Ghirnata*, Tariq Ali's *Shadow of a Pomegranate Tree*, and Nacir Khemir's film *The Lost Necklace of Tawq al-Hamama.* (Depending on audience give translations of Arabic titles

[28] For example, the Ibn Khaldun himself is many times called an Andalusian

I am Sheikh Jamal ad-Din ash-Shariji. I place my faith that reason (*'aql*) is superior to convention (*naqal*). God is Just and he does not allow his people to suffer poverty and humiliation. They spread the news about my situation and they took me to the court with four judges. After cursing and torturing me, they burned my books and put me in prison. When Timurlane took over the outskirts of the city, the Sultan of Egypt and Sham did not allow me to defend my city and nation. When Timurlane destroyed and pillaged the city, the soldiers took me to him. Among Timurlane's audiences was a group of religious leaders and intellectuals such as the Shaykh Muhiy ad-Din ibn al'Iz and the Shaykh Abdul Rahman Ibn Khaldun. They asked me about my philosophy and then when Timurlane spoke through a translator, he ordered that I be beaten and crucified until death. I was amazed that they all agreed with him.[29]

These words summarize compelling events of the play while skewering Ibn Khaldun as the person responsible for killing reason. Just as Shariji represents the public intellectual who dies in the name of reason and reform, Ibn Khaldun agrees to his murder. Ironically, the canonical figure usually portrayed as one of the most important intellectuals in Arab and Islamic history is presented in this play as part of a system that aims to stifle individuals of reason and as a self-serving intellectual in league with those in power. The irony is that this flashback provoked audience members as a world historical figure was represented as a culprit to the chronic "powerlessness" and failure of the imagined Arab nation.[30]

It is not only how book burning is depicted through Ibn Rushd and Shariji protecting threatened knowledge but Wannus' evocation of the unequivocal sense of betrayal to an intellectual, moral, and nationalist code that dominates the play. Shariji's crucifixion provokes audiences into questioning the role of the intellectual and calls attention to chronic problems in the Arab states. The ethos of shocking betrayal thus provokes a catharsis in the same way as any ending in a Greek tragedy. The play's final lines bespeak the cry of a young refugee for his mother's breast, ending the play on a futuristic note.

It is in history that this play by Wannus searches for a future for the intellectual, the Arab societies, and even the process of history itself. This article focuses on how Wannus represents a specific historic event and the dynamic historical figure of Ibn Khaldun, to create a play that is a cathartic response to the condition in the Arab states in the early 1990s. By manipulating a dynamic historical figure

---

[29] Sa'adallah Wannus, *Munamnamaat Tarikhiyah* (Beirut:Dar al Adab, 1996), 121.

[30] The fever was produced in Arab capitals like Beirut, Cairo, Tunisia, and Rabat where the play traveled during 1996–1997.

for this purpose, Wannus develops a textual structure in *Historic Miniatures* that evokes the presence of the present urgently addressing the role of the intellectual in society. Because of the importance of Ibn Khaldun's perceived "betrayal," this study reviews the history of Ibn Khaldun's involvement during the fall of Damascus and how that involvement relates to the events of the play.

Wannus juxtaposes Ibn Khaldun against three other positions in the play: At-Tadhili, who represents current trends in Islamist resistance; Sharaf ad-Din who believes in the role of the committed and active intellectual; and Jamal ad-Din ash-Shariji (follower of Ibn Rushd) who represents the imprisoned secular intellectual in exile, silenced, and hung by Timurlane. The positions of these three men counter Ibn Khaldun's role as the Arab sage who failed to resist, betrayed his people, and served the interests of those in power. He is simultaneously the intellectual who is tired of his wanderings and constantly struggling to create a home in exile.

Wannus used the relationship in the play between Ibn Khaldun and his fictional student Sharf ad-Din to dramatize his critique of Ibn Khaldun's position in history and as historian. Ibn Khaldun's role as historian is challenged not just in the plot, but also in the dramatic structure of the play. More than other Arab contemporary playwrights, Wannus employs many experimental methods in the structures of his plays, including titles, plots, scenes, and characters. His play also envisages a new way of confronting history and historiography itself.

This attention to history and historiography is apparent in the work's title. A *Munamnamah*[31] or miniature is a form of decorative oil painting that developed in the Islamic world beginning in the 'Abbassid Empire and also flourished in Persia and Mughal, India. Small, detailed paintings were usually found in books, and are distinguished by their ability to crowd a frame with a plethora of images. Now displayed all over the world, Islamic miniatures belong to different periods in Arab and Islamic history especially when prevailing religious ideology prevented the human body being represented as an image. Well known in Persian and Mughal art, the city of Damascus also has a noted tradition of replication of the miniature art form. Many books that acknowledge the miniature are dedicated to Mughal readers and Mughal leaders who revered Timurlane as one of their own. Over time, Islamic leaders have used the miniatures to strengthen their power. To examine this Arab and Islamic art form informs Wannus' general theory on history because he subverts an art form that usually is in the hands of the powerfull and gives many of the smaller details a voice in his play. This in itself represents Arab/Islamic symbols that Wannus uses to interrogate the position of Ibn Khaldun. He uses materialist symbols to deconstruct the icon of Ibn Khaldun. To study this is one way to understand, Wannus's critique of Ibn Khaldun.

---

[31] This is the singular of the Arabic form.

Linguistically, the root N-M-M of *Munamnamah* means to represent or to reveal and sometimes connotes to slander. The noun of the root *nammah* means a point of white on a black background or vice-versa. Another noun *namnamah* refers to drawing and 'inscription. "It is the writing of the wind on sand and water like the detailed drawings on a written manuscript."[32] When the adjective "historical" is combined with *munamnamah* it adds to its decorative characteristic a sense that history can be teased out of the multitude of images on the page. While the combination of history with the ornate pictures renders history in a superficial form, Wannus divides his play into three acts, and each act, or *munamnama*, is divided into many scenes that he titles *tafasil* (details), each with a theme that delves deeply into historical narrative. In fact, most scenes are not ensembles but intimate dialogues between a wide varieties of characters. Some critics have called the images "impressionistic"[33] because more than five scenes usually fill one painting, forcing a slow viewing process. Wannus might have seen *Historical Miniatures* as visual reading of historical impressions since the play attempts to elaborate and *zoom in on* these scenes. In an interview he explained:

> The historical miniatures I wanted to present combined the fine details in Islamic art and I attempted to blow them up and maybe reveal real struggles of people. In fact, my play uses the art work in an ironic way. Our history has simplified the struggles of many and marginalized their importance like the characters of the miniatures we see sold in the markets of Damascus.[34]

Hence the title is important in understanding the playwright's purpose. Wannus's structuring of his play echoes the words of Walter Benjamin:

> The true picture of the past flits by. The past can be seized only as an image which flashes up at the instant when it can be recognized and isn't ever seen again. . . . For it is an irretrievable image of the past that threatens to disappear with every present that does not recognize itself as intended in it.[35]

The Benjaminian image becomes apparent as each scene or "detail" is composed like a missing narrative fragment. The title and structure of

---

[32] Jaber 'Asfur, "Munamnamaat Tarikhiyah," *Fusul* 3, no. 121 (Summer 1998): 385.

[33] Samir 'Attiyah, *Al-Fan al-Islami bi 'Adasati Hadithah* (Damascus: Dar al-Farabi, 1999), 41.

[34] Interview with Mary Elias, *At-Tariq,* 110.

[35] Walter Benjamin, "Theses on the Philosophy of History," in *Illuminations* (Schoken: New York, 1968), 255. In thesis 7 of the above essay, Benjamin writes, "The historical materialist regards as his task to brush history against the grain." Here the author is interested in rescuing the subversive and critical periods of history that go against the "official" bourgeoisie ideology. The writers/artists in this study are involved in a process of going against the grain.

Historical Miniatures implicitly critique how Arabs and Arab historians have misrepresented their history. Hence, the play is imagined as three *art pieces* composed of a crowd of details.

Apart from the three miniatures and their details, a character named the "ancient historian" precedes each scene fretting about material matters, a common concern that continues until the end. The first lines of the play begin with the ancient historian decrying the increasing price of barley, and the exorbitant cost of rice.[36] As the play progresses, this character becomes an ironic voice that counters the tragedies and melodramas of the play, as in the third miniature when he breaks out of character to question his role, asking:

> What is my role in this catastrophe? Does the historian really matter
> if all these characters do not learn from their mistakes? Maybe my
> character must dissolve with Suad, Marwan, Ahmed, and Sharaf ad-
> Din, and not only begin to record the events but become someone
> who might change the events, but it seems I am late. It seems
> difficult to make our historian less cold and neutral, but can we be
> cold and neutral. We are getting ready for the horror that will come
> and we cannot narrate the facts without our emotions and shock.[37]

From these lines on, the historian is no longer written as separate from the action of the play. Wannus uses the ancient historian as again to subvert traditional roles found within society and Islamic tradition. As in Walter Benjamin's definition of "true" history, in which events take place in "a present which is not a transition, but in which time hesitates and comes to a standstill,"[38] Wannus brings his history to a standstill not only when the ancient historian jumps out of character but similarly with all the major characters in the play. With this Brechtian technic, Wannus questions the role of history itself in relation to the text and to the tragedy of actual historical events. The play demystifies the role of the historian and the role of the public intellectual. By writing the historian into the play, Wannus emphasizes how history and historians are integral parts of society.

Ibn Khaldun constantly insists on an intellectual's position of neutrality to his student, claiming that intellectuals and historians are not responsible for the events of history. Early in the play he tells Sharf ad-Din: "When you want to

---

[36] Wannus, *Munamnamaat*, 7.

[37] Ibid., 101.

[38] Walter Benjamin, *Illuminations* (Schoken: New York, 1968), 134. In a lecture by UCLA Professor Sam Weber, Benjamin's quotation is further connected to a differentiation between historical materialism and historiography. According to Weber, a historical materialist approaches history when history suddenly stops the constellation of ideas in order to shock people from the basic continuum of time. (Lecture notes, class on Benjamin and Traurspiel, Sam Weber, Spring Semester 1999.)

record historical events, you must control your impulses and emotions or just ignore them."[39] After his student asks how can they resist the Tatar advance, Ibn Khaldun insists: "We did not come to create prophecy, but rather to just cooperate and record."[40] Sharf ad-Din continues to challenge his teacher by asking if the intellectual's role should be to enlighten people and lead them away from decline; Ibn Khaldun insists on the neutrality of his role as a scholar.

> "An intellectual's role is to interpret events as they are, and to discover how these events happen and the underlying reasons behind them. We are outside of the process."[41]

At one point, Ibn Khaldun steps out of character to say: "If this great thinker cannot be outside the process, then how can I ignore my role as an actor in this play? Am I just an interpreter or am I someone with more power?"[42] In breaking the fourth wall of theatre, Wannus wants the audience to go back to that "standstill" in time. Wannus seems here perhaps to be influenced by Sadiq Jalal al-'Azm's theories on the roots of Arab failure. Al-'Azm has argued from a revolutionary Marxist perspective that it is necessary to bring about radical changes in life, as well as in society, because Arab intellectuals are part of the failure in their inability to break out of traditional loyalties.[43] Ibn Khaldun, the character, admits to this weakness later on the play with the question, "How many rulers must I be loyal to in order to finish my work?"[44]

Based on Ibn Khaldun's dialogues in the play, I propose rather that he is presenting Ibn Khaldun as a type of public intellectual who takes part in the failure of Arab society by proposing neutrality. Here is another example when Sharaf ad-Din continues: "Shouldn't the intellectual be responsible for enlightening the people and to guiding them out of this decline?" Ibn Khaldun responds coldly, "The role of the intellectual is to analyze reality as it is and discover the mechanisms of these events and their profound reasons." Sharaf ad-Din continues to debate and enlists the support of Artistotle and Al-Farabi, but Ibn Khaldun curiously responds, "Those intellectuals do not understand the knowledge of 'umran (civilization) and they only present internal thoughts not reality to history." Ibn haldun continues with a long monologue, claiming that those theorists were idealists and living in illusions. "Societies are not built on wishes and dreams."[45]

---

[39] Wannus, *Munamnamaat*, 12.
[40] Ibid. 33.
[41] Ibid. 43.
[42] Wannus, *Munamnamaat*, 49.
[43] Sadiq Jalal al-'Azm, *An-Naqd al-dhati ba'd al-hazima* [Self Criticism Alters the Arab Debate] (Beirut: Dar at-Tali'a, 1984), 69–88, 177.
[44] Wannus, *Munamnamaat*, 64.
[45] Wannus, *Munamnamaat*, 80.

Sharaf ad-Din's critique of Ibn Khaldun is a critique of the concept that *'umran* is trapped in an existential pessimism that frustrates human will. Even as Ibn Khaldun is cited by Edward Said as a proponent of the idea that humans create history, Wannus aims to say that this subjectivity is not enough.[46] Ad-Din's final scenes show him guarding the fortress and educating the young men, having chosen to defend his city. Sharaf ad-Din's final words to Ibn Khaldun are, "If the attributes of *'umran* are not open to the possibilities of choice, then what is left for the people? Nothing is left except apathy and the following inevitable consequences."[47] According to Azmeh, Ibn Khaldun theorized that *'umran*, which might be translated as the high point of civilization, had dissolved all across the Arab and Islamic world.[48] In Wannus's play the teacher displays a defeatist attitude, but is the student's attempts to locate an optimism that would allow intellectuals to participate in the struggles of the people. While Sharaf ad-Din exemplifies the idea that intellectuals must transcend negativity and purge pessimism to survive, Ibn Khaldun relentlessly repeats his position of neutrality in relationship to the social crisis around him.

The moral dilemmas presented by great theatre such as this, allow audiences and other intellectuals to review the social and cultural predicaments of their times. Ibn Khaldun is juxtaposed with other intellectuals. This interpretation of the play is backed up by Wannus's own statement about how his vision of the intellectual had changed from one of hubris to one of persistence and humility.[49] He believed that the role of the intellectual as critic involved "more than just an effort to exist with daily struggles, an escape from political charades, or from becoming a missionary for clichéd and closed thought or propaganda" and berated the loss of "the historical procession of intellectuals of the Nahda to those of the colonial period and then the national state" that he blamed for the defeats of the last 50 years. The intellectual "must practice his freedom and love his individuality" and realize that in being authentic he strengthens the community, which is also composed of unique individuals who did not fit the mold. "We were either ignorant or forgot that the exceptions and uniqueness both give the community a human power — not simply a collection of numbers and empty existences."[50]

Although he criticizes Arab intellectuals and other leftist intellectuals in of the Sixties and Seventies, Wannus is not demanding a neo-liberal interpretation of the role of the individual as Joseph Massad might argue, nor is he appropriating American cultural hegemony. In his review of another play by Wannus written

---

[46] Said, *On Late Style*, 6.

[47] Wannus, *Munamnamaat*, 82.

[48] Azmeh, *Ibn Khaldun: An Essay in Reinterpretation*, 34.

[49] Interview with Mary Elias, *At-Tariq* 1, no. 31 (January–February 1996), 104

[50] Interview with Mary Elias, *At-Tariq* 1, no. 31 (January–February 1996), 104.

during the same period, Massad argues that while "Wannus's critique of Arab society is admirable, his following of ready-made and interrogated Western formulae is not."[51] Wannus was clearly not following Western formulae to create *Historical Miniatures*; his sophisticated structure and well-researched story are unique. The espousal of the individual in relationship to community is not a Western concept only and the interrogation of Ibn Khaldun and the reaction to an invasion of an Arab nation transcends any efforts to play Wannus among his often correct label of Arab liberals. Massad accuses Wannus of being a neo-liberal advocating Western liberal values, an accusation that highlights a sensitive dilemma for many Arab intellectuals who risk being called pro-Western for espousing certain views. How does an intellectual critique their own culture in a time of catastrophe? Wannus responds to this idea with a larger interrogation of how communities and individuals resist.

A more sophisticated theoretical way to perceive Wannus's desire to represent the symbol of Ibn Khaldun is this suggestion by Massad is to suggest that they transcend such debates and achieved what Edward Said termed Late Style. Said delineated a specific trend in cultural production when "great artists" near the end of their lives create "work and thought that acquires new idiom.[52] Wannus first discovered that he had cancer while he was writing *Historical* Miniatures. His struggle with this disease is implicit in the work's style. "Lateness" directly concerns artists conscious of their imminent demise, as Wannus was in the 1990s. Said's posthumous text ends with Theodore Adorno's observation:

> "He [the artist] does not bring about their [objective and subjective meaning] harmonious synthesis. As the power of dissociation, he tears them apart in time, in order, perhaps, to preserve them for the eternal. In the history of art late works are the catastrophes."[53]

All of Wannus's final plays, especially *Historical Miniatures,* stage catastrophes in order to tear apart *subjective and objective concepts* in front of an audience.[54] Another important way in which Wannus's final plays fit the prerogatives of Late Style as articulated by Said is in the way in which they shatter their viewer's/reader's expectations while entertaining them at the same time. Said,

---

[51] Massad, *Desiring Arabs* Op. Cit., 375.

[52] Edward Said, *On Late Style: Music and Literature Against the Grain* (New York: Vintage, 2006). Said borrowed the term from Theodore Adorno, who applied it to the final works of classical musicians such as Beethoven and Richard Strauss.

[53] Ibid., 160.

[54] For example, in all of his last plays, the audience or readers of the play experience suicides, the collapse of families, natural catastrophes. In the play *A Day in Our Times,* which was written a year before *Historical Miniatures,* the main character commits a slow suicide by opening the gas lever in his stove. In *Malhamaat as-Sarrab,* a whole family disappears. See Sa'adallah Wannus, *al-'Amaal al-Kamilah* (Damascus: Dar al-Mada, 2002).

for example, expressed this as follows:

> This is the prerogative of late style: it has the power to render disenchantment and pleasure without resolving the contradiction between them. What holds them in tension, as equal forces straining in opposite directions, is the artist's mature subjectivity, stripped of hubris and pomposity, unashamed either of its fallibility or of the modest assurance it has gained as a result of age and exile.[55]

Through these literary techniques that exemplify Edward Said's articulation of Late Style, Wannus evokes cathartic mode of feeling in *Munamnamat tarikhiyya* that allow viewers to question themselves, their intellectuals and the power around them. The demands of Late Style are met in the urgency of this play written at the end of Wannus's life. Wannus's fever of history demands that the audience follow the lines of Jamal al-Shariji and watch out for the Ibn Khalduns of the world. Subversion and resistance in the face of catastrophe are two qualities that linger after reading the play.

In *Historical Miniatures,* the Ibn Khaldun so favored by Orientalists is subverted, Resistance, both inward and outward looking, is the prescription Sa'adallah Wannus advocates. Resistance according to this play demands this duel action—an inward personal struggle and the other outward struggle for community and political rights. The double action creates the tragedy and pathos of the play as the characters are all trying to do both at the same time. As discussed in Said's work on late style, the play present Ibn Khaldun in way that is both pleasing and disenchanting. This on some level is the resistance that only a strong theatrical performance could portray. Wannus's play becomes a foundational text for intellectuals of the postcolonial world who eloquently advocates a new vision of national identity founded on the individual praxis of each citizen without betraying the larger communities. Wannus's play shows how he believes intellectuals must look inward and recreate their own unique authenticity.

This is exemplified in the play in the actions of Sharaf ad-Din, who joins the resistance because he believes that his role as an intellectual must be dominated by hope, and affiliation to local realities. Wannus, finally, proposes in *Historical Miniatures* that we are all Ibn Khalduns when we accept the status quo and Sharaf ad-Dins when we challenge our daily positions.[56] The symbol of Ibn Khaldun is not simply torn down and represented as a power serving intellectual, his philosophy and concepts that are in and of themselves symbols of Arab/Islamic theoretical constructs become the focus of the plays actions and development.

---

[55] Wannus, *al-'Amaal*, 148.
[56] Interview with Mary Elias, 108.

The play as a whole construct shows a development to favour Ibn Khaldun's students who upholds his teacher's ideas in order to serve the larger community. The role of intellectual become a position for everyone after the catastrophe. Wannus's cultural intervention therefore asks all citizens to become part of writing history and destiny.

Another Sharp Weapon: Gender and Revolt in Arab and Jewish Editorial Cartoons, 1936-1939

Jeff Barnes*

Introduction

Editorial cartoons gained a prominent position in the Arab and Jewish press in mandatory Palestine during the 1936-1939 Arab Rebellion. Cartoons in the Jewish daily *Davar* and Arab daily *Filastin* expressed Jewish and Palestinian nationalist sentiments respectively during the revolt, negotiating the complicated and emerging contours of nationalist discourse in both communities during this key historical juncture. They played a significant role in producing and reflecting public opinion,[1] especially during the national strike that defined the first stage of the rebellion, and provide an excellent lens through which to view the emerging conflict in Palestine in the first half of the twentieth century.

In spite of their prominent role in the Arab and Jewish press in Palestine during the 1936 strike, they have received little attention from scholars.[2] In his excellent monograph on the press in mandatory Palestine, Mustafa Kabha briefly considers

---

*Jeffrey John Barnes is a Ph.D. student in the department of history at the University of Akron specializing in twentieth century Palestine. His research focuses on editorial cartoons and identity in Palestine and Israel in the twentieth century.

[1] Press argues that cartoons occupy a liminal status between their production by societal elites, who dominate print media, and their reception by a (in the case of Palestine, largely illiterate) mass audience. This tension leads to cartoons, especially in low-literacy contexts like Palestine, simultaneously producing and reflecting popular opinion. See: Charles Press, *The Political Cartoon* (London: The Associated Press, 1981), 11.

[2] Scholars have devoted considerably greater attention to Palestinian editorial cartoons in the post *Naksa* (1967) era. This is in part due to the towering influence of Naji al-Ali, Palestine's most prominent cartoonist. See for example: Sune Haugbolle, "Naji al-Ali and the Iconography of Arab Secularism," in *Visual Culture in the Modern Middle East: Rhetoric of the Image*, ed. Christiane Gruber and Sune Haugbolle (Bloomington, IN: Indian University Press, 2013), Orayb Aref Najjar, "Cartoons as a Site for the Construction of Palestinian Refugee Identity: An Exploratory Study of Cartoonist Naji al-Ali," *Journal of Communication Inquiry* 31 (July 2007), and Nadia Yaqub, "Gendering the Palestinian Political Cartoon," *Middle East Journal of Culture and Communication* 2 (2009).

cartoons in *Filastin*, especially as they relate to British censorship of the press, but offers no analysis of specific images.[3] Khalidi, who provides a cogent discussion of the role of the Mandate-era press in the project of Palestinian identity, stating that "[o]ne of the best ways to gain an understanding of the linkage between local patriotism, anti-Zionism, and Arabism in the coalescence of Palestinian identity if via study of the burgeoning press in Palestine,"[4] fails to reference cartoons at all, in spite of the fact that they demonstrate this linkage to perhaps a greater degree than the editorials he cites. LeVine's work, which highlights the importance of images, especially advertising, in the production of Palestinian identity in the Mandate-era Jaffa press, provides a brief reference to cartoons yet offers no analysis.[5] The only work entirely devoted to cartoons in both the Jewish and Arab press during the *Thawra* is Sandy Sufian's well-researched and illuminating article that draws on representation theory and demonstrates that physiognomic depictions of the body of the "Other" in Jewish and Arab cartoons during the period in question served to construct the opposing group as deviant, manipulative, uncivilized, and premodern.[6]

The present paper adds to the extant scholarship through viewing these images through the lens of gender. Editorial cartoons in the Arab and Jewish press reveal how nationalists saw the emerging conflict in Palestine primarily in gendered terms. Many of *Filastin* and *Davar*'s political cartoons employed caricatures of women to signify national difference; others referenced gendered components of Jewish and Palestinian nationalist discourse respectively. The gendered content of cartoons in both papers intersected with other signifiers including race, an imagined historical past, and national figureheads, contributing to the construction of the Jewish and Palestinian national imaginary. Decoding the multilayered signs in these cartoons, then, provides broad insight into their function and role in the Arab and Jewish presses and highlights the contentious project of Palestinian and Jewish identity during the first half of the revolt.

---

[3] Mustafa Kabha, *Writing up a Storm: The Palestinian Press as Shaper of Public Opinion, 1929-1939* (London: Valentine Mitchell, 2007), 133, 164, 190, 254, 266, 269.

[4] Rashid Khalidi, *The Iron Cage: The Story of the Palestinian Struggle for Statehood* (Boston: Beacon Press, 2006), 90.

[5] Mark LeVine, "The Palestinian Press in Mandatory Jaffa: Advertising, Nationalism, and the Public Sphere," in *Palestine and Israel and the Politics of Popular Culture*, eds. Rebecca L. Stein and Ted Swedenburg (Durham, NC: Duke University Press, 2005), 60.

[6] S. Sufian, "Anatomy of the 1936-39 Revolt: Images of the Body in Political Cartoons of Mandatory Palestine," *Journal of Palestine Studies* 37 (Winter 2008): 23-42.

Gender in the Orientalist Imagination: Editorial Cartoons and Gender in *Davar* during the Revolt

Davar, the most widely circulated Jewish daily in Palestine during the mandate,[7] contained significantly more editorial cartoons during the revolt than did *Filastin*; however, fewer of these relied on caricatures of women to express their comment. This is not to say, however, that gender did not play a significant role in the paper's discussion of the events at hand. Zionist claims were replete with gendered subtexts, even when not addressing "men" or "women" as such. Cartoons in *Davar* subverted masculinist conceptions of Palestinian nationalism, targeting discourses that projected the male head of house as emblematic of the Palestinian nation, employing a gendered "language" of nationalism to challenge Palestinian national aspirations in the Mandate.

Figure 1: "Education in Palestine," Davar, 10 December, 1936, 7.

A cartoon that appeared in *Davar* late in 1936, "Education in Palestine,"[8] illustrates how representations of Palestinian women in the Jewish press defined national difference between the two communities. In the image, a Palestinian woman reads to her child from what appears to be a copy of *al-Diffa'*, *Filastin*'s chief rival during the mandate. Sufian offers an excellent reading of how Arieh Navon (the editorial cartoonist at *Davar* during the revolt) used physiognomy in his representation of the Palestinian woman's body in the cartoon, though she does not flesh out the image's gendered implications. She sees the cartoon as a conscious attempt to extend a "…stinging appraisal of Palestinian nationalism to 'the people.'"[9]

This comes, she argues, through bringing the viewer into the Palestinian home (itself a gendered construct, a fact overlooked in Sufian's analysis). Gender therefore becomes the means through which Navon extends his critique of the Palestinian national project beyond the traditional leaders of the movement, or even the notion of Palestinian Arab identity itself (both of which were common

---

[7] The National Library of Israel's Jewish Historical Press project estimates *Davar*'s circulation as c. 15,000 at the start of the strike ("Davar," *Jewish Historical Press* < http://www.jpress.org.il/publications/davar-en.asp>).

[8] "Education in Palestine, *Davar*, 10 December, 1936, 7.

[9] Sufian, 36.

features of his cartoons during the revolt) to Palestinians as a people. By drawing the viewer into the Palestinian home, Navon ascribes to Palestinians not just the qualities of baseness and amodernity that Sufian correctly observes, but a learned violence and opposition to the Jewish people.

Navon's depiction of Palestine as a woman has deep implications for understanding the meaning of the cartoon as well as the role of gender in the nationalist imaginary during the revolt. The use of women as emblems of the nation is well established by scholars of nationalism such as Partha Chatterjee, who maintains that women form a core aspect of non-western nationalisms through signifying the "spiritual" component of the nation.[10] Fleischmann's work on women and gender in mandatory Palestine provides perspective on the gendered subtexts of the image, describing the idealized construction of Palestinian womanhood in nationalist discourse during the time of the revolt as revolving around "...educating women in order to produce men—and women—to serve the nation."[11] Navon embodies the construction of women as representative of the nation as a whole described by Chatterjee and Fleischmann, but attacks the ideal of the educated mother "serving" the Palestinian nation by depicting Palestinian women as uneducated and feeding their children the sentiments expressed in "radical" Arab newspapers such as *al-Diffa'*. The cartoon thus inverts the language of Palestinian nationalism that depicts women as "mothers of the nation," instead imagining Palestinian women as producers of future "terrorists."[12]

Navon's physiognomic portrayal of the Arab woman in "Education in Palestine" also has deep gendered implications that need to be explored. Sufian states that the woman's "...sharp tooth and the long, sharp nails of her feet and hands suggest that she is primitive and evil."[13] Additionally, she suggests that both the woman's and the child's facial features suggest "baseness and low development" and stupidity.[14] Navon projects these attributes onto the Palestinian population as a whole through employing the trope of the feminine as dangerous and deviant, a threat to and exaggeration of the norm. Additionally, Sufian points out that the woman's features convey a sense of baseness and amodernity. Nationalist movements in the Middle East claimed women "were both the vehicles and the objects of civilization...[and] a measure of the advancement or backwardness of

---

[10] Partha Chatterjee, *The Nation and its Fragments: Colonial and Postcolonial Histories* (Princeton, NJ: Princeton University Press, 1993), 3-13, 113-134.

[11] Ellen Fleischmann, *The Nation and its 'New' Women: The Palestinian Women's Movement, 1920-1948.* (Berkeley, CA: University of California Press, 2003), 82.

[12] The Jewish press in Palestine, including *Davar*, frequently employed the euphemism "terrorist" to signify any Palestinian who sought to undermine the Zionist project in the Mandate.

[13] Sufian, 37.

[14] Ibid, 37.

a culture."[15] Palestinian women thus came to signify amodernity, inauthenticity, and vice against tradition, authenticity, and morality in *Davar* specifically and in the Zionist imaginary more broadly. Couching such overtly inflammatory rhetoric in gendered caricature provided *Davar* with the means of subverting British Censorship, for as Sufian cogently remarks, cartoons enabled the shifting of subversive content from text to image, "…a form more likely to pass censorship regulations."[16]

During a period of relative calm in Palestine in 1937, Navon address the possibility of a return to violence in an untitled cartoon that undermines nationalist

projections of Palestinian manhood.[17] As Jews and Arabs in Palestine anxiously awaited the recommendations of the Peel Commission to Palestine, the cartoonist depicts an Arab man preparing for further armed insurrection. As British control of the ports and overland routes into Palestine left the rebels with few options for obtaining weapons, the man is forced to enter the British army depot and steal arms. The cartoon intends to persuade the viewer of the deviancy of the Arabs (both through the act of stealing and through exaggerating the dark skin and other physical features of the Arab), the continued threat of violence, and what Navon (and many other Zionists) perceived to be British support for the Palestine cause.

Figure 2: Untitled Cartoon, Davar, 25 February, 1937, 7.

A gendered subtext unites the overarching messages Navon projects in the image. Palestinian nationalist discourse emphasized the provider and protector role of the Arab male over his *'ard* (land) and *'ird* (woman's sexual integrity), particularly among the *fellaheen* class that comprised the majority of the rebels.[18] This masculine projection of Palestinian nationalism translated the self-sufficiency of the male head of household to the broader national project. In the cartoon, Navon subverts this discourse by highlighting Palestinian Arabs'

---

[15] Sheila Hannah Katz, "*Adam* and *Adama*, *'Ird* and *Ard*: Engendering Political Conflict and Identity in Early Jewish and Palestinian Nationalisms," in *Gendering the Middle East: Emerging Perspectives*, ed. Deniz Kandiyoti (Syracuse, NY: Syracuse University Press, 1996), 93.

[16] Sufian, 27.

[17] Untitled, *Davar*, 25 February, 1937, 7.

[18] Katz, 85-105.

perceived dependency on Great Britain. The cartoon depicts the Arab man as carrying a British officer along with the weapons, hinting not only at Navon's critique of what he viewed as British support of the Arabs, but also of the inability of Arab men to defend *'ard* and *'ird* by themselves. Additionally, the subservient position of the Arab, who is carrying the British officer, positions him in a protected (feminized) role rather than a protector (masculinized) role in his relationship with the officer, a positioning Navon maps onto the Palestinian nation as a whole in terms of its relationship with Great Britain. Thus while the cartoon does not employ the obvious gender signification present in "Education in Palestine," it nevertheless addresses gendered elements within Palestinian nationalist discourse, demonstrating how gender came to be one of the primary signifiers for the contested ground of identity and national legitimacy between Palestinian Arabs and Zionists in the Mandate.

Understanding how gender relates to nationalism in this sense is critical. While a number of scholars, such as Fleischmann, have skillfully sketched the role the so-called "women's question" played in early Palestinian nationalism, this work needs to be merged with understandings of the gendered nature of nationalism itself.[19] Editorial cartoons provide an excellent source for this endeavor, and these first two images address and demonstrate both the role of the "women's question" in Zionist imaginations of the Jewish nation as well as the gendered subtext of Jewish nationalist aspirations themselves. This stresses the significant role gender plays in constructing the nation, defining not only who belongs (and, by extension, who does not belong) within the national community, but providing the means and language through which that community is articulated.

---

[19] Hasso provides an excellent discussion of the necessity of linking to so-called "women's question" with the gendered nature of nationalism in the introduction of her article on the Women's Front in Palestine. See: Frances S. Hasso, "The 'Women's Front': Nationalism, Feminism, and Modernity in Palestine," *Gender and Society* 12 (August 1998): 442.

Figure 3: "The Concert," *Davar*, 9 January, 1938, 7.

Navon employed Orientalist visions of the Middle Eastern past to undermine Palestinian nationalist claims in a 1938 cartoon, "The Concert," which further reveals the extent to which gender was a central component in defining *Yishuv* identity vis-à-vis the Arab "Other" during the revolt.[20] The year 1938 saw a distinct rise in the violence and number of deaths during the *Thawra* and represented a transition from the violence between Arabs and Jews that characterized the first half of the revolt to an outright war of independence from Great Britain on the part of Palestinian Arabs. Further, the continued response to the Peel Commission's 1937 recommendation to partition Palestine sparked debates about the role of international intervention in the Palestine question. This context factors into the cartoon in which British Prime Minister Neville Chamberlain, Italian Prime Minister Benito Mussolini, and German Chancellor Adolph Hitler perform a concert for an Arab man reclined in a position reminiscent of European Orientalist paintings of the Ottoman harem. Chamberlain sings alone while Mussolini and Hitler work together in an apparent attempt to seduce the Arab. Anxious about the role Great Britain, Italy, or Germany could play in supporting the Palestinian Arabs against the Zionist cause, Navon highlights the dangers that competition between these powers could play in the region.

The central signifier in the image is an updated version of the Middle Eastern harem, an institution that had fascinated European travelers to the Middle East for centuries. While Navon's cartoon certainly intends to depict the baseness and amodernity of the Arab (as did the previous two cartoons) through the use of visual signifiers such as a camel and tent (primitive transportation and housing), it is the gendered invocation of the harem that makes this image so profound. The positioning of the various characters in the image coupled with the music motif draws the viewers' minds to Orientalist paintings of the Ottoman harem. Pierce maintains that the west (which includes, by extension, Zionist immigrants to Palestine, most of whom at this point came from Europe, and who carried with them the cultural baggage of European thinking about the Orient) is "…heir

---

[20] "The Concert," *Davar*, 9 January, 1938, 7.

to an ancient but still robust tradition of obsession with the sexuality of Islamic society. The harem is undoubtedly the most prevalent symbol in Western myths constructed around the theme of Muslim sensuality."[21] In European mythology, the harem was understood to be characterized by the sultan's participation in orgiastic sex that "…became a metaphor for power corrupted.[22] These themes, part of a broader tradition of European thinking about the Middle East, are brought to the surface in "The Concert."

Navon's cartoon intentionally employs the European construction of the institution of the harem to convey meaning. The Palestinian man, fulfills the role of the Ottoman sultan, while the others—Chamberlain, Hitler, and Mussolini— are meant to call to mind the women of the harem. A frequent feature of Orientalist paintings of the Ottoman harem is music, a motif that is replicated by the "women's" performance in the cartoon, which provides further evidence of Navon's use of harem imagery. The man sits and smiles, obviously pleased by the performers. Again, Navon makes use of European perceptions of the harem to communicate his message through this cartoon, relying on the (decidedly incorrect, as Pierce and others have so aptly demonstrated) dominant European belief that the women of the harem lacked any agency. Thus the gendered imagery makes Navon's point clear: while the great powers of the world sought to influence the unfolding conflict between Jews and Arabs in Palestine to their favor they were, in fact, mere pawns in the hands of the Arab leadership in Palestine. Further, as the harem signified corruption in the European imagination, Navon assigns an immoral, underhanded nature to the support he perceived that world powers offered to Palestinians. There is little doubt that Navon was conscious of the fact that British officials monitoring *Davar*'s content would see that cartoon and understand its message. Important, too, is the fact that "The Concert" demonstrates once again how the *Yishuv* applied gendered discourse to craft its political message in the context of the revolt, this time merging gender with historical imaginations of the Arab past.

---

21 Leslie P. Pierce, *The Imperial Harem: Women and Sovereignty in the Imperial Harem* (Oxford, Oxford University Press, 1993).
    22 Ibid, 3.

The Threat of Esther: Editorial Cartoons and Gender in *Filastin* during the Revolt

Filastin, the most widely circulated Arab daily during the mandate,[23] contained relatively few editorial cartoons during the Arab revolt compared with *Davar*, a fact no doubt influenced by the disproportionate focus of British censorship on the Arab press during the mandate, including a total ban on cartoons in the Arab press in August, 1936.[24] As was true for *Davar*, *Filastin*'s editorial cartoonist was European; however, the paper's chief editor, 'Issa al-'Issa, ostensibly developed the ideas that the cartoonist drew.[25] As a result, the cartoons reflect al-'Issa's penchant for stinging critiques of Zionism and in particular Jewish immigration.[26] *Filastin*'s cartoons frequently represented Palestine and Zionism with women and, like *Davar*'s use of gendered discourse to delegitimize Palestinian national aspirations, sought to undermine masculinist visions of the "New Jew" that were central to the identity Zionist community in Palestine during the Mandate.

Figure 4: "Jewish Immigration Protected by British Bayonets," *Filastin*, 15 June, 1936, 1.

An editorial cartoon featured in Filastin during the early stages of the revolt, "Jewish Immigrants Protected by British Bayonets," underscores the gendered nature of Palestinian and Jewish nationalism during the revolt.[27] A chief aspect of the Jewish Renaissance of the late-nineteenth and early-twentieth century, of which Zionism was a byproduct, was the desire to counter centuries of

---

[23] Citing the 1937 Peel Commission findings, Kabha estimates *Filastin*'s circulation at the same time to be c. 4-6,000 (Kabha, 155). Literacy rates were considerably lower among Palestine's Arab population (see Ami Ayalon, *Reading Palestine: Printing and Literacy, 1900-48* (Austin, TX: University of Texas Press, 2004), 16-17. While newspapers were read aloud in cafes to disseminate news to the illiterate (Khalidi, 26), cartoons provided a "text" that could be "read" by all. This is reflected in the fact that *Filastin*'s cartoons were always displayed prominently on the first page of the paper, where they would capture the attention of this audience, whereas cartoons in *Davar* were placed at random places throughout the paper. This was especially important during the 1936 strike, which was based on mass participation on the part of the *fellahin*.

[24] Kabha, 176.

[25] Sufian, 29.

[26] LeVine, 60.

[27] "Jewish Immigration Protected by British Bayonets," *Filastin*, 15 June, 1936, 1.

antisemitism through presenting a masculinized "new Jew" for the twentieth century. Sheila Hannah Katz describes this discourse in the first half of the twentieth century as follows:

The bronzed, muscular farmer/soldier 'New Man' was the Zionist alternative to his stooped, intellectual and victimized diaspora predecessor. Jews associate the *galut* [the idea of a nation forcibly removed from its homeland and subjected to foreign rule] with characteristics deemed negatively feminine such as being passive or vulnerable victims. In a sense, men felt relegated to [and sought to overcome] being symbolic women, that is, subjects of degradation and abuse by other men of dominant cultures. The 'New Man' of Zionism was supposed to throw off the powerlessness of two thousand years.[28]

Al-'Issa directly targeted this idea of Jewish self-sufficiency in Palestine in "Jewish Immigration Protected by British Bayonets," replacing the masculinized "New Man" of the Zionist movement with masses of Jews immigrating to Palestine who were entirely dependent on the benevolence, intervention, and protection of Great Britain.

The cartoon depicts three boats of Jewish immigrants arriving in Palestine (most likely in Jaffa, the port-city in which *Filastin* was headquartered), ready to begin their new life in the Mandate. This immigration, which increased dramatically in the 1920s and 1930s, was a central component of the Zionist dream and was a principal factor of the emerging conflict between Jews, Arabs, and the British in Palestine. However, contrary to Zionist claims of self-sufficiency and masculinity, al-'Issa imagines the immigrants as unable to achieve this dream on their own. Rather, they require the protection and assistance of the British mandatory government in Palestine. Though fleeing persecution, they remain passive victims, the feminized stereotype that Zionist organizers sought to counteract. Indeed, the cartoon pictures one British soldier for every Jewish immigrant. The entire picture clashes with the vision of Palestine being drawn by Zionist leaders in Europe as a land where labor and self-sufficiency were emblems of the renewed Jewish people.

This commentary employs gender to make several different points. Firstly and chiefly, it critiques and undermines one of the central gendered aspects of early twentieth century Jewish nationalism, namely the projection of self-sufficiency and masculinity, effectively claiming that the Jewish immigrants remained unable to support their own aspirations and thus continued to be in a feminized state. In doing so, it projects Jewish immigration to Palestine as unnatural, as something that, rather than provide for the uplift of the Jewish people, creates a new set of troubles for them. Secondly, the cartoon overtly critiqued British policy regarding Jewish immigration and presented it as a betrayal of former promises made to

---
[28] Katz, 87.

the Arabs (a subject explored in more depth in the last cartoon considered, "The Man of the Two Wives"), further echoing the gendered nature of the production of nationalist and anticolonialist discourse during the revolt. The obvious use of force by the British in the cartoon to facilitate Jewish immigration is an affront to the honor of Palestine, a violation of the motherland. Palestinian nationalists (as did many of their counterparts throughout the world) often imagined the land as a woman, and the forceful actions of the British in the cartoon are intended to represent an assault on her honor. As immigration became the chief cause for conflict between Arabs and Jews in Palestine, the land became an increasingly sacred (and feminized) concept. Thus, a cartoon such as "Jewish Immigration Protected by British Bayonets" visualizes a violation of the land by the Zionists aided by the British, further demonstrating how editorial cartoons during the *Thawra* made use of gender to express nationalist sentiment. As was the case with Navon in *Davar*, it is certain that al-'Issa developed the concept of this and other cartoons fully conscious of the fact that British officials would be reading it.

Filastin's cartoonist also used more overtly gendered imagery to convey al-

Figure 5: "Another Sharp Weapon," Filastin, 10 July, 1936, 1.

'Issa's critique of Zionism's relationship with Great Britain in "Another Sharp Weapon."[29] She[30] depicts Zionism as a Jewish woman named Esther whose arm wraps suggestively around British colonial secretary William Ormbsy Gore as their hands clasp tightly together. Standing behind her is Chaim Weizmann, then president of the World Zionist organization. The inclusion of Weizmann in the cartoon comes as no surprise, as Sufian argues that the use of well-known Zionist figures served to signify not necessarily the specific person, but rather the group they represented,[31] in this case the World Zionist Organization, one of the principle groups promoting immigration to Palestine. The dialogue, which was considerably more extensive

---

[29] "Another Sharp Weapon," *Filastin*, 10 July, 1936, 1.
[30] While al-'Issa developed the concept of all of *Filastin*'s cartoons during the strike, he employed a European woman (about whom little else, including her name, is known) to draw the images. See: Sufian, 27.
[31] Sufian, 26.

than any text contained in *Davar*'s cartoons, reveals that she is trying to convince Ormbsy Gore to include the "seizure of Arab lands" as part of the policy of collective punishment employed by the British during the Arab revolt.

Al-'Issa deliberately represents Zionism, and more specifically Zionist influence on British policy, as a woman, employing the nationalist trope of women as threat to the nation. The caricature does not simply intend to undermine and feminize the Zionist construct of the 'New Jew' as "Jewish Immigration Protected by British Bayonets" did. Rather, al-'Issa draws on the artistic device of woman as dangerous, seductive, and seditious—a trope whose salience partially owed to emerging fears about the changing roles of women in society—to express al-'Issa's concerns about the relationship between the British government (in this case represented by the colonial office) and Zionism. In this sense, al-'Issa borrows on the same caricature of a woman embodying the threat posed to the nation as did Navon in "Education Palestine." Taken together, then, the two cartoons demonstrate how discourse surrounding the "women's question" in the first half of the twentieth century translated into nationalist discourse through using women to signify the nation.

Esther's suggestive clothing and posture draw on the imagined threat of unchecked female sexuality to signify the dangerous result of Zionism's relationship with world powers such as Great Britain. The cartoon, based on many Palestinians fear that Great Britain was decidedly pro-Zionist,[32] was meant to convey that Zionist promises to Great Britain were illusory (hence the use of the imagery of an affair) at best, and a threat to British national interests at worst. Esther—representing the World Zionist Organization's influence on British policy—was, as the cartoon's title reveals, a sharp weapon. In a similar manner, gendered discourse itself became "another sharp weapon" in the hands of nationalist cartoonists in *Filastin* and *Davar*, a primary means of organizing nationalist discourse and delegitimizing Jewish and Palestinian nationalisms respectively.

---

32 Indeed, this fear was somewhat founded, for there was a significant camp within British foreign policy that argued for British support of Jewish immigration to Palestine as in Great Britain's best interests. See: Tom Segev, *One Palestine Complete: Jews and Arabs under the British Mandate* (New York: Henry Holt and Co., 2000), 381.

The man of the two wives

الرجل ذو المرأتين

JOHN BULL :— my Lord, I married first an
Arab women and then a Jewess and for the
last 16 years I have had no peace at home ...
THE ARCHBISHOP :— How did you manage
to have two wives, are you not a Christian ?
JOHN BULL :— It was the pressure of the
Great war, my Lord ...

مقول يول : اني تزوجت أولاً امرأة عربية ثم تزوجت ثانياً
امرأة يهودية ومنذ ١٦ سنة حتى الآن والسلام والهناء منفيان ...
أمير الأساقفة : وكيف تزوجت اثنتين أأنت مسيحي ؟؟
.... الحرب الكبرى

Figure 6: "The Man of the Two Wives," Filastin,
25 July, 1936.

One of the last cartoons to appear in *Filastin* in 1936, "The Man of the Two Wives," provides a final example of how al-'Issa employed gender in his cartoons.[33] While "Jewish Immigration Protected by British Bayonets" undercut masculinized components of Zionist discourse and "Another Sharp Weapon" signified the threat of Zionist influence on British policy with a seductress, "The Man of the Two Wives" uses caricatures of two women, one Jewish, one Arab, to define Jewish and Palestinian national identities respectively. The scene depicts John Bull (the iconic caricature of the British Empire) bringing a dilemma before the archbishop. He tells the archbishop that he "…married first an Arab woman and then a Jewess and for the last 16 years I have had no peace at home." The dialogue belies Great Britain's schizophrenic relation with Zionism and Arab nationalism vis-à-vis the Palestine question. Bull's sixteen-year dilemma draws the viewer back to the 1920 San Remo negotiations that laid the foundation for the British Mandate in Palestine. The marriages represent the competing elements of British foreign policy circles that were torn between throwing Britain's support behind the Arabs or the Zionists. The reference that Bull married first and Arab then a Jewess reflects the contradictory claims the British government made in the McMahon-Hussein correspondence (1915) and the Balfour Declaration (1917). Bull excuses this impropriety by blaming the pressures of "the Great war [sic]". Finally, the archbishop informs John Bull that his only option for peace is to divorce his second wife, the Jewess, and live in harmony with his first wife. Thus, the image challenges Great Britain to maintain the promises it made to the Arabs first and to remain loyal to them.

The cartoonist depicts both the Arabs and the Zionists in female form, but the difference between the two women is telling. Al-'Issa's portrayal of the Jewish woman is similar to his caricature of Esther in "Another Sharp Weapon." Her clothing is anything but traditional, signifying licentiousness and her "outsider" status in Palestine. Her cigarette conveys immorality and vice. Al-'Issa's portrayal relies on the signifying role of gender to translate these characteristics

---

[33] "The Man of the Two Wives," *Filastin*, 25 July, 1936.

84

to the newly arrived Zionists as a whole. His concept of the Arab woman relies on the opposite use of women in the nationalist imaginary, namely their portrayal as emblems of the nation. In contrast to the worldly image of the Jewish wife, Bull's Arab wife is presented with an aura of purity. She dons the *thobe*, the traditional garment worn by women in Palestine, representing an authentic connection to the land and its heritage. In place of a cigarette, she holds a dove, demonstrating the purity of the Palestinian people. Al-'Issa maps discourses of peoplehood (i.e. the fragmented and intersecting components of identity) onto women's bodies, demonstrating Chatterjee's characterization of women as representatives of the non-material aspects of nationalism, and further cements the importance of gendered discourse for the broader Palestinian nationalist project.[34]

Linking Gender, Cartoons, and the Revolt in Jewish and Arab Editorial Cartoons

The above cartoons demonstrate the extraordinary degree to which the competing projects of Jewish and Palestinian identity were articulated along gendered lines during the Arab Revolt of 1936-39 in Palestine. Zionist identity in the Mandate relied heavily on the masculinized concept of the "New Jew," which emphasized self-sufficiency and manual labor as central attributes of the Jewish national home in Palestine. Cartoonists in the Arab press actively sought to counter this image by depicting the Zionist colonization of Palestine as entirely dependent on the intervention and protection of the British, as shown in "Jewish Immigration Protected by Jewish Bayonets." This categorization undermined the Zionist ideal of self-sufficiency, effectively feminizing the Zionist project in Palestine. On the other hand, Palestinian nationalism emphasized the connection between a man's ability to protect his '*ard* (land) and '*ird* (woman's sexual integrity). Cartoons in the Jewish press in Palestine during the revolt played on this construction, depicting Arab men as unable to defend their nation without the help of an outside party (as was the case in the second cartoon considered) and thus incapable of preserving either land or women's purity. From this it is possible to see the level to which both Palestinian and Jewish nationalism relied on gendered discourse during the revolt.

Further evidence that highlights the important role of gender in the contest between Jewish and Palestinian nationalism during the revolt can be found

---

[34] The use of women and women's clothing to signify national difference in the Middle East has a history that predates the 1936 revolt in Palestine. See: Palmira Brummett, "Dogs, Women, Cholera, and other Menaces in the Street: Cartoon Satire in the Ottoman Revolutionary Press, 1908-11," *International Journal of Middle East Studies* 27 (1995): 433-460; Fatma Müge Göçek, "Political Cartoons as Site of Representation and Resistance in the Middle East," in *Political Cartoons in the Middle East*, ed. Fatma Müge Göçek (Princeton, NJ: Markus Wiener Publishers, 1998).

through examining the use of gendered signifiers in the cartoons in the Arab and Jewish press in Palestine during the era. Cartoons in *Davar* and *Filastin* used women's bodies to represent both national groups, signifying modernity and tradition, authenticity and illegitimacy, deviance, danger, and seduction. In the language of nationalism, women can be used to represent either a threat to the nation (as can be seen in "Another Sharp Weapon," "Education in Palestine," and the caricature of the Jewish woman in "The Man of the Two Wives") or emblematic of the nation itself (such as the portrait of the Palestinian woman in "The Man of the Two Wives"). Cartoonists also drew upon gendered misrepresentations of the region's past, including the Ottoman institution of the imperial harem, to address present concerns, as was demonstrated in "The Concert."

Understanding the different ways in which cartoonists employed gender in *Filastin* and *Davar* during *al-Thawra* leads to several important conclusions. Firstly, this study nuances the extant scholarship on the critical role played by the press during the first part of the revolt. Cartoons were featured in the Arab press in Palestine only during the summer of 1936,[35] highlighting the relative strength of the Arab press during this period. British censorship efforts that began in earnest in August of 1936 severely weakened the press' role, a process mirrored by the waning of the Palestinian national movement in general. The Jewish press, however, continued to pick up steam, as did the broader effort toward the creation of a Jewish national home in Palestine, which is reflected in the prominent role played by cartoons in *Davar* throughout the rest of the revolt.[36] Secondly, understanding gendered signification in these cartoons reveals the process through which Palestinian and Jewish identities were taking shape in the period leading up to the establishment of the state of Israel and the contemporary Palestine conflict. Thirdly, these cartoons demonstrate one means through which nationalism translated into popular culture. The discourse of nationalism emerged in the nineteenth century in many ways as a bourgeois-oriented affair. Pop-culture mediums such as cartoons translated this discourse across class lines and contributed to the project of "inventing traditions" within the Jewish and Palestinian national projects in particular. An example of this can be found in the tendency of both press' cartoons to

---

[35] Cartoons reappeared in *Filastin* late in 1939, well after the conclusion of *al-Thawra*; however, post-revolt cartoons served a different function in the paper than did those published during the revolt. See: Jeffrey John Barnes, "Visualizing the Emerging Nation: Jewish and Arab Editorial Cartoons in Palestine, 1939-48," in *Postcolonial Comics: Texts, Events, Identities*, ed. Binita Mehta and Pia Mukherji (New York: Routledge, 2015), 171-186.

[36] An untitled editorial in *Filastin* from 13 August, 1936, captures differing treatment of the Arab and Jewish press by the British government in Palestine, stating that "Anyone following recent developments can see that the government acts only as proposed by the Jewish newspapers…They are those that called for the suspension of Arabic newspapers…"

emphasize images of belonging and exclusion, which as has been demonstrated was often achieved through the use of gendered imagery.

The 1936-39 Revolt in Palestine was a critical turning point for both Palestinian and Jewish nationalism. British reprisals against Palestinian Arabs effectively terminated the Palestinian national movement and contributed to the collapse of the Arab economy in Palestine. The Zionist movement, however, emerged from the revolt not only unscathed, but more resolute in its determination to establish a Jewish national home in Palestine. Zionists would build on this strength and take advantage of the fact that Great Britain was able to invest few resources in Palestine during World War II to lay the foundations for the eventual establishment of the state of Israel in 1948 and subsequent displacement of nearly one million of the territory's original inhabitants. The revolt-era cartoons in *Filastin* and *Davar* capture this contentious period in caricature. Cartoons provided an important medium through which emerging notions of Palestinian and Jewish identity could be negotiated during the transformative events of 1936-39.

This was especially true in the case of Palestine, whose rule population remained largely illiterate and thus dependent on visual, rather than textual sources of information. However, cartoons also were also indispensable to the Zionist project in Palestine. The press, including cartoons, provided a platform for disseminating Zionist identity in the Palestine to the thousands of Jewish arrivals to the territory every year. In the cartoons of both national communities, gender intersected with other markers of identity to mediate these competing and emerging nationalisms.

Taken together, these cartoons demonstrate the degree to which nationalist discourse was gendered during the Palestinian revolt and demonstrate the utility of the editorial cartoon for understanding this period. While some scholars have addressed these cartoons (either briefly, as Kabha did, or extensively in the case of Sufian), none have yet examined the critical role gender played in them. Indeed, the cartoons in both papers between 1936 and 1939 make it apparent that nationalism not only makes use of gender, but rather is dependent on gender. Contested territorial claims, the role the international community (especially Great Britain) played in determining the final status of Palestine, and the national identity of both Arabs and Jews relied on gendered constructions disseminated through mediums such as editorial cartoons, and such debates could not have gained the same meaning without gender. Finally, it is important to note that these gendered cartoons reveal how the conflict in Palestine between Jews and Arabs unfolded as part of a historical process and is not merely an age-old hatred between two communities. Rather, just as the conflict came into being historically (and quite recently) and was articulated on gendered lines, it has the potential to end just as suddenly, as activists now use gender in a variety of ways to combat violence between both groups.

Book Reviews

Edited by Nadia Barsoum

Middle East, South Asia and North Africa

TURKEY: The Insane and the Melancholy, by Ece Temelkuran translated by Zeynep Beler .London: Zed Books, 2016. 296 pages. Temelkuran identifies a long-running culture of repression and authoritarianism that has plagued Turkey throughout its history, a culture she traces back to the fall of the Ottomans and the continued climate of denial around the Armenian genocide. But, she firmly believes there is still a strong voice of dissent in Turkey, and she argues that the Gezi Park protests of 2013 represented a glimmer of hope that has not yet been fully extinguished and may still grow to rejuvenate democracy in the country. Providing unique insight into Turkey s ongoing political turmoil, this is a timely look at a country that is caught at the center of many of the changes and much of the turmoil of the Middle East today.

THE DEATH OF A NATION and the FUTURE of THE ARAB REVOLUTION by Vijay Prashad, California: University of California Press 2016, 238 pages. The heart of this book explores the turmoil in Iraq, Syria, and Lebanon—countries where ISIS emerged and is thriving. It is here that the story of the region rests. What would a post-ISIS Middle East look like? Who will listen to the grievances of the people? Can there be another future for the region that is not the return of the security state or the continuation of monarchies? Placing developments in the Middle East in the broader context of revolutionary history, *The Death of the Nation* tackles these critical questions.

THE ROLE OF MEDIA IN PROMOTING REGIONAL UNDERSTANDING IN SOUTH ASIA edited by Priyanka Singh. New Delhi: institute for Defence Studies & Analyses, 2016.256 pages.This book focuses on a range of issues relating to media-ownership, impact of social media, media narrative, nationalist bias, state control, envelope journalism, threat from non-state actors, and a host of other such issues. There is a consensus that the media has vastly enhanced its capability to mould and shape public perception and opinion with the revolution in communication technology in recent decades.   .

ISLAMIC CIVILIZATION IN THIRTY LIVES: THE FIRST THOUSAND YEARS by Chase F. Robinson. California: University of California Press 2016, 272 pages. Beginning in Islam's heartland, Mecca, and ranging from North Africa and Iberia in the west to Central and East Asia, Robinson not only traces the rise and fall of Islamic states through the biographies of political and military leaders who worked to secure peace or expand their power, but also discusses those who developed Islamic law, scientific thought, and literature. What emerges is a fascinating portrait of rich and diverse Islamic societies. Alongside the famous characters who colored this landscape—including Muhammad's cousin 'Ali; the Crusader-era hero Saladin; and the poet Rumi—are less well-known figures, such as Ibn Fadlan, whose travels in Eurasia brought fascinating first-hand accounts of the Volga Vikings to the Abbasid Caliph; the eleventh-century Karima al-Marwaziyya, a woman scholar of Prophetic traditions; and Abu al-Qasim Ramisht, a twelfth-century merchant millionaire.

IN THE LAND OF A THOUSAND GODS: A History of Asia Minor in the Ancient World by Christian Marek, translated by Steven Rendall, NJ: Princeton University Press 2016, 824 pages. This book is not only for specialist but for the general reader interested in history. It included genealogies, maps, and illustrations, as well as dates, translations. The lush chapters begin with prehistoric times and proceed through the Stone Age, the Bronze Age, the Persian Empire, Hellenization, and finally the establishment of Constantinople (present-day Istanbul) under imperial Rome. The best passages explore famous mysteries, like the legendary city of Troy, and illuminate the Anatolian roots of classical art, literature, and science. For example, Herodotus, "the Homer of history," was born in Asia Minor to a Carian-Greek family, his work representing the synthesis of Greek and Middle Eastern cultures.

EVEN IF IT AIN'T BROKE YET DO FIX IT: Enhancing Effectiveness through Military Change by Vivek Chadha. New Delhi, India, 191 pages. The book concludes that given the wide spectrum of threats faced by the Indian Army, as also most major armies across the world, attempts at understanding military change only through the prism of conventional wars could be misleading. It suggests that change need not only be revolutionary to enhance effectiveness. It could be both revolutionary and evolutionary, top-down and bottom-up. While effective change is primarily major in conventional conditions, it could well be tactical and yet make a substantial impact in sub-conventional scenarios. Finally, the book reinforces its conclusions through a survey of officers from the Indian Army, to highlight existing limitations that need to be corrected in order to better innovate and adapt in pursuit of effective military change.

NO BORDERS: The Politics of Immigration Control and Resistance by Natasha King. London, England, Zed books 2016, 196 pages. No Borders is a vital reading for anyone interested in how to make radical alternatives a genuine possibility for our times. Raising crucial questions about the nature of resistance, King shows that, far from being an idle fantasy, the ideal of a world without borders is very much of the here and now. She examines where and how activists have so far succeeded, and the difficulties that are currently holding them back.

FREEDOM WITHOUT PERMISSION: Bodies and Space in the Arab Revolutions edited by Frances S. Hasso and Zakia Salime. North Carolina Durham: Duke University Press 2016, 294 pages the contributors of this volume reveal the centrality of the intersections between body, gender, sexuality, and space to these ground breaking events. Essays include discussions of the blogs written by young women in Egypt, the Women2Drive campaign in Saudi Arabia, the reintegration of women into the public sphere in Yemen, the sexualization of female protesters encamped at Bahrain's Pearl Roundabout, and the embodied, performative, and artistic spaces of Morocco's 20 February Movement. Conceiving of revolution as affective, embodied, spatialized, and aesthetic forms of upheaval and transgression, the contributors show how women activists imagined, inhabited, and deployed new spatial arrangements that undermined the public-private divisions of spaces, bodies, and social relations, continuously transforming them through symbolic and embodied transgressions.

INCARNATIONS A HISTORY OF INDIA IN FIFTY LIVES by Sunil Khilnani, New York : Farrar, Straus and Giroux 2016, 450 pages Khilnani explores the lives of 50 Indians, from the spiritualist Buddha to the capitalist Dhirubhai Ambani --lives that light up India's rich, varied past and its continuous ferment of ideas. Khilnani's trenchant portraits of emperors, warriors, philosophers, poets, stars, and corporate titans--some famous, some unjustly forgotten-bring feeling, wry humour, and uncommon insight to social dilemmas that extend from ancient times to our own. As he journeys across the country, and through its past,the author uncovers more than just history. In rocket launches and ayurvedic call centres, in slum temples and Bollywood studios, in California communes and grimy ports, he examines the continued, and often surprising, relevance of the men and women who have made India - and the world.

RETURN TO THE SHADOWS: The Muslim Brotherhood and An-Nahda since the Arab Spring by Alison Pargeter. London: Saqi Books 2016. Pargeter's book offers a devastating portrait of Muslim Brotherhood groups in Egypt, Tunisia, and Libya. For those in Western policy and academic circles who continue to tout the Brotherhood as a moderate or mainstream Islamist movement, The Arab Spring heralded a profound shift in the Middle East, bringing to power Islamist movements which had previously been operating in the shadows. But navigating their respective countries through difficult and painful transitions ultimately proved too challenging for these forces, and, just as suddenly, the Brotherhood was dramatically overthrown in Egypt and left severely weakened in Libya. In Tunisia, An-Nahda managed to pull itself through the crisis, but its failure to articulate and deliver the hopes and aspirations of a large section of Tunisian society damaged its credibility.

SOUTH ASIAN SURVEY

Editor: **ERIC GONSALVES**, *Indian Council for South Asian Cooperation, New Delhi*

Biannual: **March, September**

Given the rapidly changing political and economic climate in South Asia, the major aim of **South Asian Survey** is to enhance an understanding of South Asia among the countries of the region and beyond. It carries contributions from scholars, policy-makers, civil servants, diplomats and journalists, providing in-depth analyses with a multidimensional approach. Although issues of national and regional concern are debated primarily from the perspectives of politics, economics and international relations, **South Asian Survey** also draws upon insights from the fields of culture, history and mass communications. The journal is a biannual publication of the Indian Council for South Asian Cooperation, New Delhi.

HIGHLIGHTS OF VOLUME V

Kalyan Raipuria Foreign Economic Policy: Challenges and Perspectives

Indra Nath Mukherji India's Trade and Investment Linkages with Nepal: Some Reflections

Krishna B Bhattachan Nepalese Perceptions of European Donors' Approaches to Poverty Reduction in Nepal

Devendra Kaushik India and Central Asia: Renewing a Traditional Relationship

P Stobdan Regional Issues in Central Asia: Implications for South Asia

Rehman Sobhan Regional Cooperation in South Asia: A Quest for Identity

Arif A Waqif Pakistan's Regional Concerns: Emerging Dimensions

A M Vohra India and Pakistan: Towards Better Understanding

RECENT SPECIAL ISSUE

• SAARC's First Decade: Looking Ahead

SAGE Publications
Post Box 4215, New Delhi 110048
2455 Teller Road, Thousand Oaks, California 91320
6 Bonhill Street, London EC2A 4PU

JOURNALS FROM SAGE

Tired of political correctness, conventional wisdom and received ideas? See below.

Middle East Policy

Volume VII   February 2000   Number 2

THE GULF COOPERATION COUNCIL
Joining the Global Rules-based Economy:
  Challenges and Opportunities for the GCC   CECILIA KLEIN / ABDELALI JBILI /
       KEVIN R. TAECKER / SHAFFEQ GHABRA
GCC Financial Markets   MOHAMED JABER
Saudi Arabia's Will to Power   JOSEPH A. KECHICHIAN

PEACE OF THE BRAVE?
The Palestinian Refugees   DONNA ARZT / DON PERETZ
Syria, Israel and the Peace Process   MARTHA NEFF KESSLER
The Future Israeli-Palestinian Relationship   MOSHE MA'OZ / GHASSAN KHATIB /
       HERBERT C. KELMAN, ET AL.

JERUSALEM
Academic Myths and Propaganda   GHADA HASHEM TALHAMI
The Revised Condominium Solution   JOHN V. WHITBECK
American Rabbis' Statement on Sharing   JEWISH PEACE LOBBY

LIBYA
U.S. Policy toward Qadhafi's Libya   RONALD E. NEUMANN
Qadhafi's Changed Policy   MARY-JANE DEEB
The Prospect of Islamic Succession   RAY TAKEYH

The Politics of Morocco's "Fight against Corruption"   GUILAIN P. DENOEUX

Published by the MIDDLE EAST POLICY COUNCIL

Rotten Trade

Global integration of markets and growth in international trade have exposed a system of trade in legal goods with dangerous consequences.

Articles in the Winter-Spring 2002 Issue include:

What is Rotten Trade?
A dialogue with Jagdish Bhagwati
Laudable Failure: The United Nations Small Arms Conference
Aaron Karp
Corruption in a Globalized World
Peter Eigen
Stolen Goods: Coltan and Conflict in the Democratic Republic of Congo
Dena Montague

Islams

The resurgence of Islam as a political force has done more than challenge the prevailing system of international relations; it has called into question the entire paradigm of universalism.

Articles in the Summer-Fall 2001 Issue include:

Islamic Identity: Myth Menace, or Mobilizer
Jilian Schwedler
Religion, Politics, and Security in Central Asia
Shireen Hunter
Indonesia's Mild Secularism
K.H. Adurrahman Wahid
Struggles Behind Words: Shariah, Sunnism, and Jihad
Radwan Masmoudi
Foreign Policy Debate: Propaganda, the Satans, and other Misunderstandings
John L. Esposito, Robert Satloff, and Shibley Telhami

Annual Subscriptions
$26.00, individuals, $17.00, students, $63.00, institutions

Single Issues
$17.00, individuals, $38.00, institutions

Send Orders to:
The Johns Hopkins University Press
Journals Publishing Division
P.O. Box 19966, Baltimore, MD 21211-0966
To place an order using Visa or Mastercard, call toll-free 1-800-584-1784, FAX to 410-516-6968, or send Visa/Mastercard orders via email to jlorder@jhunix.hcf.jhu.edu.

The Korean Journal of Defense Analysis

ublisher
un Yong Song

ditor-in-Chief
)ong Joon Hwang

xecutive Editor
:yongmann Jeon

ssociate Editors
`aeho Kim
oon-Lai Cho

ssistant Editor
eunghoon Ham

opy Editor
:raig Campbell

A Biannual Journal of Defense
published by
The Korea Institute for Defense Analyses

The Journal (ISSN 1016-3271) is circulated to institutions and analysts concerned with Northeast Asian and relevant international security affairs. In order to request a copy of the Journal or to be placed on the Journal's mailing list, please write to KIDA.

The Journal invites the submission of articles, commentary, and conference reports on all Asian security issues, with a focus on Northeast Asia. Manuscripts should be submitted in duplicate to the Executive Editor and will not be returned. They should include notes and do not normally exceed 25-30 typewritten double-spaced pages in length. Please also include a two-page, double-spaced abstract of the article as well as a one-page, double-spaced curriculum vitae. If in any way possible, a 5¼ inch MS-DOS, or 3½ inch MS-DOS or Macintosh diskette would be greatly appreciated. The Korean Journal of Defense Analysis reserves the right to edit for space.

The views expressed in the Journal are those of the individual contributors and do not necessarily represent those of KIDA.

Subscription orders and correspondence should be sent to:

The Korean Journal of Defense Analysis
Office of Research Cooperation
Chung Ryang P. O. Box 250
Seoul 130-650, Korea
Tel: (82)(02) 9611-652/9611-334: Manuscripts
9611-662: Subscriptions & Advertising
Fax: (82)(02) 965-3295

US RELATIONS WITH AFGHANISTAN AND PAKISTAN
The Imperial Dimension

HAFEEZ MALIK

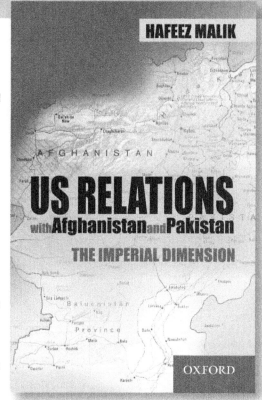

This is an analytical study of US power, described as an imperial system as against a policy of imperial conquest. An imperial system regulates the affairs of the world politically, economically and in international trade.

Against the background of US power, the author examines US relations with Afghanistan and Pakistan highlighted by the fact that both states have forged new asymmetrical alliances with the US. These alliances not only serve the strategic interests of the US but also protect the security interests of both Afghanistan and Pakistan. Both nations face a serious challenge from the violence and terror unleashed by the Al Qaeda movement, which is now in a position to destabilize the two neighbours. The present alliance with the US is aimed at defeating the terrorist movement initiated by Al Qaeda and provides the basis for national development of both the developing states.

About the Author

Dr Hafeez Malik is Professor of Political Science at Villanova University, USA, where he has taught since 1961. In 1973 he established the American Institute of Pakistani Studies, and in 1992, with Dr Sakhawat, the Pakistan American Congress. He has been since 1977 the Editor of the *Journal of South Asian and Middle Eastern Studies*. His area of specialization includes US foreign policy toward Russia and Central Asia, South Asia, and the Middle East, on which he has published and lectured widely.

Oxford University Press is a department of the University of Oxford. It furthers the University's objective of excellence in research, scholarship, and education by publishing worldwide.

Available at:
www.oup.com/pk
www.oup.com/us
www.amazon.com

CPSIA information can be obtained
at www.ICGtesting.com
Printed in the USA
BVOW11s0738200217

476564BV00003BA/3/P